The Life of Abraham

People <u>IN</u> THE BIBLE

Malcolm Maclean

DayOne

Here is biblical exposition that is text-anchored, soul-nourishing and life-directing. As Malcolm Maclean interprets the Abraham narratives, he is never more than an inch away from their claims on your thinking, worship and obedience. You will find that he seeks to make his treatment encouraging rather than exhaustive, that he is informed yet unafraid to make independent judgements, and that he is eager to bring you to the feet of Jesus, where you should be anyway.

Dale Ralph Davis, Minister in Residence, First Presbyterian Church, Columbia, SC, USA

Malcolm Maclean's classic exposition of Abraham's life (Gen. 12–25) highlights a historically and redemptively important section of the Od Testament. Important because, first, The New Testament commends the Old as 'written for our instruction' (Rom. 4:23–24, 15:4; 1 Cor. 10:11); second, Abraham is named over seventy times in eleven New Testament books, including all four Gospels; and, third, Abraham receives significant commentary in the New Testament 'Hall of Faith' (Heb. 11:8–10, 17–19). This superb Old Testament biographical sketch will stimulate the mind and stir the soul to a greater devotion and obedience to our Lord Jesus Christ.

Richard Mayhue, ThD, Research Professor of Theology Emeritus, The Master's Seminary, Sun Valley, CA, USA

Finally, a theologically sound, immensely engaging and utterly practical account of the life of Abraham! In these pages Maclean exalts the covenant faithfulness of God, and masterfully demonstrates how the pattern of Abraham's life is not so different from our own as twenty-first-century Christians. Indeed, as 'strangers and exiles' who are ever struggling against the powers of this 'present evil age', we too, by grace through faith in Christ, are eagerly anticipating 'a better country, that is, a heavenly one'. Well written and deeply challenging, this book is a must-read for God's pilgrim people!

Jon D. Payne, Minister, Christ Church Presbyterian, Charleston, USA

ISBN 978-1-84625-361-4

Unless otherwise indicated, Scripture quotations are from The Holy
Bible, English Standard Version (ESV), copyright © 2001 by Crossway
Bibles, a division of Good News Publishers. Used by permission. All
rights reserved.

British Library Cataloguing in Publication Data available

Published by Day One Publications
Ryelands Road, Leominster, HR6 8NZ
Telephone 01568 613 740 FAX 01568 611 473
email—sales@dayone.co.uk
web site—www.dayone.co.uk
North America—email—usasales@dayone.co.uk

Cover design by Rob Jones, Elk Design
Printed by TJ International

To the congregation of Greyfriars
and Stratherrick Free Church of Scotland,
who have shown great love to me.

Contents

God appears to Abraham (Acts 7:1–4)

B y any account of the biblical story, Abraham is one of its most crucial characters. Although he lived long before the Israelites became a nation, he was regarded as one of the fathers of their nation. His influence continues in the New Testament, with the writers of the apostolic church asserting that he was their spiritual father. Yet if we had seen Abraham before his encounter with the Lord, we would never have imagined that he would become such a prominent person in the Bible. The reason for this is obvious: in those days Abraham was not a believer in the true God. Instead he was an idolater, as explained by Joshua, the leader of the Israelites whom God chose to lead them into the promised land:

And Joshua said to all the people, 'Thus says the LORD, the God of Israel, "Long ago, your fathers lived beyond the Euphrates, Terah, the father of Abraham and of Nahor; and they served other gods. Then I took your father Abraham from beyond the River and led him through all the land of Canaan, and made his offspring many"' (Josh. 24:2–3).

So how did this idolater become a member of the people of God?

Surprisingly, the answer to this question is not found in the Old Testament. It is the case that Genesis 12 describes a call of God to Abraham, but that call was given to him in Haran many years after he had received his first call from God. The description of his original call is given in the final address of the first Christian martyr, Stephen:

Brothers and fathers, hear me. The God of glory appeared to our father Abraham when he was in Mesopotamia, before he lived in Haran, and said to him, 'Go out from your land and from your kindred and go into the land that I will show you.' Then he went out from the land of the Chaldeans and lived in Haran. And after his father died, God removed him from there into this land in which you are now living (Acts 7:2–4).

So Abraham received two calls from God regarding a journey to an unknown land. One call he received in Ur and the other call he received later in Haran.

Ur of the Chaldeans?

Where did Abraham come from? One of the great cities of the ancient world was called Ur, and it was located near to the modern Iraqi city of Naziriyah in southern Mesopotamia. It was the main city of the Sumerian civilization, a very advanced culture. Many scholars have assumed that was the place where Abraham lived. If it was, then Abraham would probably have enjoyed a good standard of living there. In recent years, however, evidence has been found of the existence of another Ur, in northern Mesopotamia, the area inhabited by the Chaldeans—which would explain why it was called Ur of the Chaldeans.

From one perspective, it does not matter which of the Urs is the correct one. Yet there is one point to note: in the past many scholars doubted the biblical account because they had no evidence for calling the southern city by the name of 'Ur of the Chaldeans'. Yet archaeology has provided evidence for the existence of a smaller town of that name in the Chaldean area of northern Mesopotamia. The obvious deduction to make is that sooner or later archaeological discoveries will vindicate the biblical accounts, and there is no need for us to doubt what the Bible says even on the issues of history and geography.[1]

God appears to Abraham

One clear point from Abraham's initial experience is that the Lord often selects an unlikely person in order to bring about an important stage in his purposes. Abraham was an unlikely choice whether he lived in the southern Ur or the northern Ur. He was an idolater, which is not the background we would expect of one who would become a prominent person in the development of God's kingdom. Yet is this not the way God often works? The history of the church is filled with examples of unlikely people who became his servants. We can think of Saul of Tarsus, the fierce persecutor of the early church. Or we recall Martin Luther, the dedicated monk desperate to find God in a dead church and whom God had purposed to use as a catalyst in the Reformation. Then there is George Whitefield, whose mother ran a public house in Gloucester, where George performed his acting skills to amuse the audience. John Newton is another unlikely character whom God used to bring hope and guidance to thousands. We can add D. L. Moody, whose employment was selling shoes in a Boston shop. From this list we can deduce that we should never be surprised when God uses an unexpected person in his work. In fact, we should be surprised when he uses those of whom it is anticipated.

A second point is that God knew where Abraham was, whether in the southern or northern location. We are not told how old Abraham was when God appeared to him in Ur. When that took place, it was the first time Abraham thought about the true God—but it was not the first time God thought of him. In fact, God had had his eye on Abraham for every second of his life, watching him, working on him, developing his natural talents, giving him bodily strength. Without Abraham being aware of it, the Lord had been at work, anticipating the time when he and Abraham would have their first conversation.

A third point concerning the experience of Abraham is that the God of glory appeared to him. We are not given any details of this experience. It was probably what is called a 'theophany', a temporary appearance of God in human form. In what way this took place cannot be described, except to suggest that it left a permanent effect on Abraham. God was to appear later to Abraham, and on these occasions Abraham had no difficulty recognizing the Lord.

When we recall that God is infinite, we can deduce that it was an act of surpassing condescension when he appeared to Abraham the idolater. The Lord was so determined to have Abraham become his servant that he was willing to humble himself to bring that about. Sometimes we ask ourselves what God would have to do in order for us to worship him. Perhaps he could throw a few universes into existence before our eyes. I would certainly be impressed, but I think I would want to worship such a God from a distance. But if, after making those universes, the almighty God was to take on a form whereby he could draw near to me and speak to me, then I would be not only amazed by his power but also attracted by his condescension, and I would worship him with respect and intimacy.

However God appeared to Abraham, it caused the idolater immediately to change his practice of worship. The information he discovered about God made God the priority in his life. This explains why it was straightforward for Abraham to do what God requested of him.

Fourth, we can note the demand that God made of Abraham. It was a divine call requiring separation, and a divine promise assuring security. Perhaps we are puzzled as to why Abraham was required to leave his land and family. Why could he not stay where he was and witness to God in Ur? One suggestion is that his environment and his family were riddled with practices connected to worship of the moon. As long as Abraham remained in Ur, he would be tempted by his connections to make compromises. It was for Abraham's own spiritual good, and for the spiritual prosperity of his descendants, that God separated his servant from the surrounding culture.

Obedience to this divine command also required an element of sacrifice on the part of Abraham. Yet the Lord assured him that the recompense of his dedication would be great. He would receive territory from the Lord, land that would be his by divine gift. Abraham was called by God to respond in faith, which he did; but his faith was governed by the visit he had received from God and the words he had heard spoken to him by the Lord. Therefore, Abraham explained the situation to his family and immediately left Ur, with some of his family going with him.

Lessons for ourselves

Above we mentioned God choosing unlikely people through whom to fulfil his purposes. Perhaps we think that God would never use us. Strangely, such an outlook is an expression of pride because it assumes that God is not able to use us. The fact is that we do not know what God will use us for, yet it is the case that he can use us to do something for him. We should offer ourselves to him, whatever our age, to serve him wherever he wishes to place us. He may give us a ministry of prayer that will change the destiny of nations. He may give us the opportunity to influence in a spiritual way a person who will later become one of God's giants.

We also noted that the Lord knew where Abraham was and came down to his level. In a far more profound way, God has also done this for us. We could say that God's own experience on this occasion was a foretaste for him of his incarnation later on. The Lord of glory became a man in order to reveal to sinners the infinite, transcendent God. The One who formed the universe took on our frame and came and spoke to us about God. What great humility was displayed by Jesus throughout his earthly journey! And he has retained his humanity, which means that he will in the future, throughout the endless ages, be able to tell us about God and his greatness.

We also noted that it was the sight of the God of glory that stimulated Abraham to begin his journey. To us has been given a greater sight, the sight of a suffering Saviour taking our place on the cross of shame. The story is told of Count Zinzendorf, the founder of the Moravian church. One day, he saw a painting of the cross and beneath it the words, 'All this I did for thee; what hast thou done for me?' Zinzendorf was so affected by the cross of Christ that he gave his vast wealth for the spread of Christian missions.

In addition, we have the sight of the exalted Saviour, reigning triumphantly for ever. His is the eternal glory, and he desires that sinners share it with him for ever.

Again, as with Abraham, Jesus comes to us with a call to separate from what is sinful and with a promise of secure territory. He calls us out from an environment of spiritual danger and from the prospect of eternal destruction. We are urged to leave a world of sin and begin a journey to the heavenly city, and we are urged to begin the journey now. Jesus gives us the promise of secure territory as an incentive to make the choice. The territory is not some acres in the Middle East, but the new heavens and new earth, the heavenly country, the land of limitless dimensions.

Abraham made the right choice, and we shall see in later chapters how he got on. Suffice it to say for the present that he is now in the presence of the God of glory who came to him in Ur of the Chaldees. And the patriarch still marvels at the condescension of the One who became a man in order to reveal God.

NOTES

1   'Abraham's family is from Ur of the Chaldees. For many generations the only Ur that has been known to modern scholars is the famous Sumerian city on the southern Euphrates. It has been somewhat of a mystery why this southern city would be referred to as Ur of the Chaldees—since at this time the Chaldeans were settled primarily in the northern section of Mesopotamia. An alternative was provided when textual evidence from Mesopotamia began to produce evidence of a smaller town by the name of Ur in the northern region, not far from Haran (where Terah moves his family). This town could logically be referred to as Ur of the Chaldees to differentiate it from the well-known Ur in the south. This would also explain

why Abraham's family is always seen as having its homeland in "Paddan Aram" or "Aram Naharaim" (24:10; 28:2, descriptions of northern Mesopotamia between the Tigris and Euphrates).' From 'Ur of the Chaldees', Gen. 11:28, in John H. Walton, Victor M. Matthews and Mark W. Chavalas, *The IVP Bible Background Commentary: Old Testament* ((electronic ed.); Downers Grove: InterVarsity Press, 2000).

Abraham's second call (Gen. 12:1–5)

W e saw in the previous chapter that God had initially called Abraham when he lived in Ur of the Chaldees. In response to the call Abraham had left that city, along with his father Terah and other family members. They travelled as far as Haran, a region that today is on the border of Turkey and Syria. There they settled down—for how long we cannot say, although we are informed that this second call occurred after Terah had died. So we can assume that the delay had a connection with Terah.

Was Abraham a backslider in Haran?

The second call that Abraham (then known as Abram[1]) received was virtually the same as the first call. He was told to leave his situation and his family and go to an unknown location. There he would prosper under the hand of God, and eventually he would become a blessing to the whole world (Gen. 12:1–5). The point to note is that when God gives a second call, he does not adapt his original call.

This feature is found in the experience of many in the Bible who received a second call from God in a specific way. One of the best-known examples is Jonah, who initially refused God's call to go to Nineveh, but who discovered that attempts to divert God's intention will not work. Another example is Peter, although his second call from God came after his repentance over his denial of Jesus. A third person is Mark, who failed in his calling as an apostolic assistant, was later restored and was regarded as very useful by the person whom he had failed, the Apostle

Paul. To that list of stalwarts we can add Abraham, the father of the faithful.

Why did he delay? We are not told, so every suggestion is just a guess. The usual assessment is that Abraham was distracted from fulfilling his calling through disobedience to God's revealed will. It is suggested that he should have left his family behind in Ur and not allowed them to come with him. In his study of Abraham, F. B. Meyer, who wrote many books assessing Bible characters, is adamant that Abraham was hindered by his father in the life of faith. That may be true, but if it is we must ask why he was willing to take Lot with him after his second call. It is true that Lot caused Abraham a lot of problems, but those problems were caused by Lot's attitude and not by Abraham's kindness in being willing to take him along. I am not aware of any biblical passage that suggests Abraham was wrong to look after family members who were willing to travel with him.

In contrast to the suggestion that Abraham was hindered by Terah is the idea that the older man was converted as a result of the divine message received by his son when in Ur. John Calvin wrote,

In short, Moses records this oracle, in order that we may know that this long journey was undertaken by Abram, and his father Terah, at the command of God. Whence it also appears, that Terah was not so far deluded by superstitions as to be destitute of the fear of God. It was difficult for the old man, already broken and failing in health, to tear himself away from his own country. Some true religion, therefore, although smothered, still remained in his mind. Therefore, when he knew that the place, from which his son was commanded to depart, was accursed, it was his wish not to perish there; but he joined himself as an associate with him whom the Lord was about to deliver. What a witness, I demand, will he prove, in the last day, to condemn our indolence![2]

In between these two views is that of Matthew Henry, who regards Terah as a picture of many who set out for Canaan but do not get there, who are not far from the kingdom of God, but not in it. The problem with Henry's suggestion is that it makes Terah's physical death a reason for his spiritual death, whereas the account can be read as indicating he was an old man who was prepared to travel to the earthly promised land in order to enjoy the blessings of God, but found himself enjoying heavenly ones instead. For what it is worth, I prefer Calvin's interpretation and do not regard Abraham's time in Haran as delay caused by disobedience.

If the delay was not caused by disobedience, why was Abraham hindered in getting to the promised land? It is at least possible that he was delayed by family responsibilities. His father Terah was willing to go with him and went as far as Haran. As mentioned earlier, Abraham stayed there until his father died, and we have no means of knowing how long they remained there (Abraham was seventy-five when he left Haran): it may have been a month, a year or a decade. Perhaps the delay was caused by Terah's inability to travel any further, and the group had to wait there until he passed away. Similarly, some people receive a call from God to work for him but are hindered from doing so by legitimate circumstances in God's providence. Yet when the situation is resolved, the Lord sends his call again and recommissions them, as it were, for the task. Such providences are not permanent barriers; instead they are ways of God saying to us, 'Wait on my time.'

We do not know which option is right, or whether either is correct. I would lean towards the second option, mainly because the biblical accounts don't condemn Abraham for this action. Where there were definite failures in his life, the accounts mention that he was in the wrong. Also, with others who received a second call—such as Jonah, Peter and Mark—we are told what their sinful action was that affected the initial call. A third possible argument that supports the idea that Haran was not a bad experience for Abraham is that God allowed him to take with him the various items he had accumulated there. If they were illegitimate things he had collected during a time of backsliding, I do not think the Lord would have allowed Abraham to hold on to them.

Abraham's experience teaches us that God is often not in a hurry. In past generations, when life was slower, this reality was often not a difficulty. Would-be missionaries knew that they would have to wait several years before they would reach their fields of labour. Even in domestic circumstances, people were used to waiting (e.g. a husband might go abroad to find a place for his family to live, and they knew that it might take several years for him to send word that he had found it). One of the biggest difficulties facing us today is the sense of immediateness that marks our society, whether it is sending messages or travelling to other places. They are difficulties because God has not changed his methods of preparation. He is often prepared to wait until a particular time he has fixed. Today, if God has decided that the suitable date for a person to go to serve him in a particular place is in March 2020, it makes no difference to his plans that a dozen planes will be flying there every day until then. He will arrange the best time, which usually is when his chosen servant is ready.

In passing, we can note another way which shows that God was not in a hurry. Abraham was seventy-five when he left Haran with God's renewed call in his heart, yet he was going to have to wait twenty-five years before God fulfilled the next stage in his promise, the birth of his descendant. Abraham would be one hundred when Isaac was born (Gen. 21:5).

An important passage in the Bible

If someone were to ask you what the most important passage in the Bible was, you might give several options in reply. You might say that Genesis 1–3 is very important because it describes the creation of the universe and the entrance of sin into the world. Or you might choose the last two chapters in the book of Revelation, because they depict the wonders of heaven. Or you might choose prophecies such as Isaiah 53, because it combines God's ability to predict the future and the details of what happened to Jesus on the cross. Of course, the question is not a valid one because it is not possible to say which is the most important passage in the Bible.

Nevertheless, we must insist that there are key moments in the Bible in the unfolding of God's purpose of mercy. These help give us a framework by which we can understand what God was doing. In this regard, we can mention the new world after the flood, the new people of God after the exodus, and the church after the day of Pentecost as key moments in God's plan for his kingdom. To them we need to add this passage in Genesis 12, because it is not too much to say that the remainder of the Bible is an exposition of what is declared in these verses.

For example, God promises to Abraham that he will have a specific country and that he will be the ancestor of a great nation. In a sense, these two details summarize the rest of the Old Testament, because it is largely about what took place in the land of Canaan, and it describes what happened to the nation of Israel, the descendants of Abraham.

The promise to Abraham extends beyond these historical Old Testament references, through the New Testament and down all the centuries since then. Abraham heard a promise that is connected to you and me, although he had no idea that we would exist. He was told that through him all the nations of the world would be blessed. This is a reference to the coming of the Saviour, the Descendant of Abraham, the man who stayed in Haran for a short time.

This promise of God to Abraham was one of universal blessing, which means that God separated him in order to bring blessings to others. Abraham was told to isolate himself so that through his obedience to God others would receive a blessing. This principle is not as strange as it may sound. God still makes the same demands of his people. He says to them, 'Draw near to me in prayer, either by yourself or with others, and pray to me about giving spiritual blessing to other people.' What Abraham did physically, we are asked to do spiritually: to separate in order to procure a blessing. The opposite is also true: if you don't separate, you deprive others of a blessing.

Three blessings we share with Abraham

The promise made to Abraham involves spiritual blessings. What are these favours that God is going to give to others? There are many, but three in particular arise out of the promise here.

First, Abraham himself is a reminder that acceptance with God is not based on our works, but on faith in the promised Deliverer. I suppose that Abraham could point to his lifestyle of obedience as a means of obtaining God's favour. Yet we know that Abraham failed God often. So even his dedicated life, in which he made many a sacrifice for the cause of God, was not the means by which he became right with God. Instead he had to trust in the One whom God promised would yet come to provide salvation. And when Jesus came, he testified about Abraham to the Jews in John 8:56: 'Your father Abraham rejoiced that he would see my day. He saw it and was glad.' Abraham looked ahead and trusted in what Jesus would do on his behalf.

We have to do the same. Our good works are of no use as far as becoming right with God is concerned. We have to do what was done by David Dickson of Irvine, a well-known Scottish preacher who died in 1662: 'As for myself, I have taken all my good deeds, and all my bad deeds, and have cast them together in a heap before the Lord; and have fled from both to Jesus Christ, and in him I have sweet peace.'[3]

In Romans and Galatians Paul uses the experience of Abraham to set out the great truth of justification by faith alone. Abraham depended for his salvation entirely on the work of Jesus Christ. He is not in heaven now because he lived a life of devoted obedience to God's call; he is there because he committed his soul by faith into the care of the future Saviour.

Second, this divine promise to Abraham points to the fact that in this world we have no final resting-place. The Bible itself says that Abraham did not regard the possession of the land of Canaan as being the full meaning of this great promise from God. Paul says this in Romans 4:13: 'For the promise to Abraham and his offspring that he would be heir of the world did not come through the law but through the righteousness of faith.' Abraham saw beyond the earthly territory to another world, 'to the city that has foundations, whose designer and builder is God' (Heb. 11:10). In other words, Abraham saw in this aspect of the promise the greater reality that one day there would be a new heaven and new earth in which he as an heir of God would live for ever. This reality recognized by Abraham has yet to be fulfilled, but one day it will be. May each one of us be there and join 'Abraham, Isaac, and Jacob in the kingdom of heaven' (Matt. 8:11).

Third, God promised Abraham that his name would be vindicated: 'I will bless those who bless you, and him who dishonours you I will curse' (Gen. 12:3). Abraham, who went forth in faith upon God's promise, travelled under the assurance of God's protection from enemies. Yet I think this detail also stretches across the ages down to the judgement seat. Here is a reminder that God will one day deal with people according to how they have treated his people. Is this not what Jesus says in the parable of the sheep and the goats in Matthew 25? The test is clearly stated:

And the King will answer them, 'Truly, I say to you, as you did it to one of the least of these my brothers, you did it to me.' ... Then he will answer them, saying, 'Truly, I say to you, as you did not do it to one of the least of these, you did not do it to me.' And these will go away into eternal punishment, but the righteous into eternal life (Matt. 25:40, 45–46).

These three great promises were only the first of many that the Lord gave to Abraham. Throughout his life, he would have reflected many times upon them. Today he can testify from heaven that these promises have within them far greater prospects than even the greatest believers on earth can imagine. But they have been given to us as well as to Abraham in order to help us journey as pilgrims to the heavenly city.

NOTES

1 I have used the name Abraham throughout this book, for the sake of simplicity.

2 John Calvin, *Calvin's Commentaries*, Volume 1: *Genesis* (Grand Rapids, MI: Baker, 1999 [repr.]), p. 342.

3 Cited in John Howie (1775), *The Scots Worthies*, chapter on David Dickson (Edinburgh/London: Oliphant, Anderson & Ferrier, 1871 [repr.]), p. 295.

Making progress (Gen. 12:6–20)

T he writer of Genesis passes over the details of Abraham's journey from Haran to Canaan. All we are told is that a successful journey was made. The impression is given that nothing unusual happened during that period in Abraham's life. He left Haran and travelled to Canaan aware that the Lord had promised to guide him there. So, although the author does not record any individual events, he does inform us of two details: that God keeps his word, and that some stages in the spiritual journey can be rather mundane. Every day Abraham just had to keep going, and often this is the way for us too.

His experience depicts the reality of the Christian life. Often nothing unusual happens: we engage in the same activities day by day, and we have to keep going. Our comfort from these stages depends on our perspective. We can look at these times and say that nothing is happening, or we can look at them and say, 'God is leading me onwards and keeping his word. One day he will take me to the destination he has planned.'

The mundaneness of our spiritual experience should not cause us to think that there are not many significant milestones ahead. Often these times are days of preparation in which God gets us ready for what is ahead. Many people have looked back to periods spent out of the limelight as days when God taught them many things. For example, we cannot begin to estimate what Paul discovered during the period he spent in Arabia (Gal. 1:17). Therefore we should value quiet periods as important ones preparing us for more dramatic situations.

This passage divides into two sections. The first section tells how Abraham built two altars to the Lord, one at Shechem and the other at

Bethel. The second section relates the story of a conspicuous failure in the life of Abraham, when he was willing to compromise his wife in order to save his own skin. At the very least, this incident tells us that the person whom God has chosen can perform unexpected actions, and it is a reminder that the one whom God intends to use still sometimes engages in sinful behaviour.

Building altars to the Lord (vv. 6–9)

At first glance, we may see nothing noteworthy in this activity of Abraham apart from indicating that he was a very devout person. Such, no doubt, was his character, yet I suspect that the author of Genesis wants us to see that Abraham's actions were in fact significant, and that for at least two reasons.

To begin with, we need to discover what was taking place at Shechem and the location near Bethel as far as the inhabitants of Canaan were concerned. Verse 6 mentions a particular tree at Shechem and that gives us a clue. Trees were used in places of pagan worship because it was thought that the noise of the wind rustling through them was the voice of the gods, and this noise would be interpreted by a soothsayer. The name 'Moreh' means 'oracle-giver' or 'teacher', and this tree points to Shechem as a place of pagan worship or divination.

'Bethel' is the name Jacob gave to the city of Luz after the Lord appeared to him when he was on his way to his uncle's home (Gen. 28:19). Moses is using this name because he is writing the story of Abraham long after Jacob gave the name to the city, although when Abraham passed by the city it was called Luz. Modern writers use the same method today when they say that something happened near a particular place, even though that place may not have existed when the incident happened. Archaeologists have discovered that pagan worship took place on a ridge on the east of Luz (Bethel). Abraham did the same thing there that he had done at Shechem: he built an altar to the Lord in places where pagan worship took place. Why did he do this?

Abraham was saying more than that he was a worshipper of the true God. If that was all he wanted to say, he could have built an altar anywhere and worshipped alongside it. Instead he was stating that he was there as the representative of the true God and that the land of Canaan would not be a place of idolatry for ever. These altars built by Abraham were both an expression of his confidence in the word of God and a challenge to those who worshipped the false gods. The altars symbolized the advance of God's kingdom in a hostile environment.

Abraham's actions depict how we should live today in a culture in which all kinds of religions are on display. Of course, we don't erect altars in order to state who we are and who our God is. Instead we tell the story of Jesus Christ. As with Abraham, we have a choice as to where we can tell the story. He could have built his altar far away from the pagan shrines—and likewise we can tell the gospel far away from where the modern idolatries are taking place.

Yet if we have confidence in the gospel we will tell the story of Jesus right where other things have first place. These other things can be anything in the lives of people that takes the place Jesus should have— ranging from actual religious places through to apparently legitimate things such as sports events or musical concerts. Telling the story of Jesus will always challenge the listeners as to their way of life.

The author informs us that Abraham received divine consolation and encouragement from God before erecting the altar at Shechem (v. 7). There is a very basic lesson here for us: before we do anything for God, we should have fellowship with God. Sometimes we need extra-special encouragement from the Lord, especially when we are about to do something that is very dangerous or for the first time. This altar at Shechem seems to have been the first made by Abraham since the God of glory appeared to him in Ur of the Chaldees. His God was not insensitive to the weaknesses of his servant and drew near to encourage him. This was not the last time that the Lord would do this for Abraham. Spending time with God before doing something for God brings spiritual energy and courage.

The appearance of the Lord to Abraham was a 'theophany': God appeared in a human form. This is the third recorded appearance of God to Abraham in this way. He was being assured that the Lord was with him as he progressed through the land. It is likely that these theophanies were appearances of the Son of God in particular before he took on a permanent human form.[1]

It is important for us to note that courage was needed by Abraham. These religious sites had not been abandoned by their users; Moses stresses in verse 6 that the Canaanites were still in the land. Abraham did not choose a derelict site in which to erect his altars. Instead, in the presence of the Canaanites, close to where they worshipped their false gods, Abraham revealed that he was a worshipper of the true God. Of course, he knew that God was all-powerful; yet his courage did not come from his knowledge alone. Like all who have dared to do things for God, Abraham obtained courage by spending time with God.

CLAIMING THE LAND OF PROMISE

Another lesson stands out from the choice of locations mentioned by the author. Shechem and Bethel were in different parts of the country. It is hard not to deduce that Moses is pointing out that Abraham was inspecting the land in which God had promised to bless him. The patriarch was journeying through the land discovering what God had in store for him and his descendants in a physical sense.

In a similar way, God has given to his people a region in which he will bless them. This area is not defined in geographical dimensions. Yet, just as there were different places in Canaan for Abraham to observe and enjoy, so there are places in the spiritual country for God's people to visit. Each Christian is called to live the life of an explorer of God's country.

We can imagine Abraham sitting down near Shechem and saying to himself, 'All that my eyes can see belongs to me.' God would whisper to him, 'You have a lot more than what your eye can see. But in order to see it, Abraham, you have to move about the promised land.' Therefore, he had to get up and travel around, visiting different places. Similarly, we can be content with one of God's blessings instead of exploring them all. For example, we can so enjoy looking at the blessing of justification that we fail to look at other spiritual blessings, such as adoption or the ministry of Jesus in heaven on behalf of his people. We have to get our souls on the move and visit other blessings and discover there too that God has good things for us.

In concluding this section we can note that the two features of Abraham's activities—the tent and the altar—illustrate the basic outlook of those living for heaven. The tent indicates that believers are people on the move, travelling to a definite destination which they have not yet reached. The altar symbolizes that they journey as those who are devoted to God.

Going too far (vv. 10–20)

Things had been going well for Abraham. Then his circumstances changed and he found that he was in the midst of a famine. Perhaps he had never been in a famine before. So when he heard that there was food in Egypt he decided to leave the promised land and go there. Very likely he saw other people doing this and he followed their example. This seemed to be the common-sense approach to life.

It seems that Abraham did not realize he was being tested by God as to whether or not he would depend on God when things were no longer easy. This was probably the first test he faced, so his response is understandable. It was not going to be the last test he faced, and no doubt he learned some painful lessons from this incident. As we think of this incident in Abraham's life, we should never be surprised at how quickly we can move from the heights of devotion to God to the depths of denial of God. Usually, it takes only a little test.

The narrator's description tells us that Abraham made a big mistake in going down to Egypt. In what ways can we see this?

First, Abraham lost his courage. He did not lose it a few miles into Egypt after seeing hostile looks on the faces of the inhabitants; he lost his courage as soon as he made the decision to go down to Egypt. On the surface his choice seemed like common sense, yet below the surface it was an expression of distrust in God. He did not seem to grasp that the God who had led him from Ur could take care of his needs in the promised land. The moment we stop trusting in God we will lose the provision of divine courage and boldness that he usually gives.

Second, Abraham lost his compassion. In a way that is completely indefensible, he was prepared to let his wife suffer in order to save his own skin. He became selfish and concerned only about himself. It was better for Sarai to be in a famine than in a harem, but since Abraham was thinking only about himself, he was prepared to let her suffer. Probably his actions would have been deemed reasonable by the standards of the culture, and perhaps he was wanting to be known as her guardian rather than her husband. In such a scenario, anyone wanting to marry Sarai would have to ask him. Such a worldly way of escape would be successful in the main, and perhaps Abraham forgot that there was one man in Egypt who did not have to ask permission for his actions: Pharaoh.

It is intriguing that several years later Abraham repeated the same strategy when he again left the promised land and went to Gerar (Gen. 20). Is there a hint here that our particular personal weaknesses will always show themselves when we step away from the Lord's revealed will?

Third, Abraham lost his discernment. We can see this in the way he was willing to accept the gifts that Pharaoh gave him in exchange for Sarai (v. 16). He became prosperous at the prospect of her danger. And he does not seem to have felt any guilt. Yet he was paying a heavy price for his riches, for he was being blinded by his circumstances. Prosperity is not an infallible guide that we are walking according to the Lord's will. If Abraham deduced it was, then he was in real spiritual trouble.

THE FAITHFULNESS OF GOD

Fortunately for Sarai, and for Abraham, the Lord had not abandoned her and he protected her in the dangerous position her husband had placed her in. This is wonderful information because it is a reminder that the Lord is always faithful to his covenant arrangements. As Paul reminded Timothy, 'if we are faithless, he remains faithful—for he cannot deny himself' (2 Tim. 2:13).

Yet the faithfulness of God did not mean that he kept quiet about Abraham's sin. Usually, when a person repents of his or her sin to God, it is the end of the story unless there are public aspects to the sin. In this situation, Abraham had to endure public humiliation (vv. 18–20). The rebuke was not a sign of Pharaoh's nastiness, but of his concern for natural justice. There was little point in Abraham building an altar in Egypt.

Instead, Abraham had to return to the last place where he had shown spiritual life: Bethel (13:3), where he had built an altar expressing his dependence on the Lord. We have no idea whether or not the famine was over in Canaan. Whether or not it was, Abraham had now realized that a spiritual relationship with God is more important than temporal security. Similarly, many Christians have to return to their Bethels, to a life marked by devotion to Jesus. They have to repent of trying to find security and satisfaction in other things. The good news is that the way to recovery is a certain and sure path along which they can travel confessing their sins.

Chapter 3

This path always lead to spiritual restoration, to the resumption of their walk with God.

NOTES

1 For a helpful discussion of theophanies as appearances of the second Person of the Trinity, see James E. Borland, *Christ in the Old Testament* (Tain: Mentor, 1999).

Rediscovering the path to spiritual success (Gen. 13:1–18)

W e noticed in the previous chapter that Abraham had begun his life in Canaan with spiritual confidence, expressed by his determination to indicate to the peoples of the land that from now on it belonged to him through a gift from God. This he had done by building altars to the true God in the vicinity of pagan shrines, an action that revealed both his courage for God and his loyalty to God. Yet this period of spiritual progress had been stopped by his decision to go down to Egypt during the famine. That decision had been caused by a lack of trust in God, a response which can be found among even the best of Christians when they face a new situation, never mind in a spiritual novice, which Abraham was at that time.

Nevertheless, Abraham discovered that his God was still working on his behalf in providence, even if he was embarrassed at having his deception made public by Pharaoh, who sent him back to his own land. In passing we can note that some of the most embarrassing words that Christians can receive come from worldly people who tell the Christians that they should be living in a spiritual territory other than that in which the worldly people live.

In any case, Abraham was now on his way back to where he should be, and in his journey we have a picture of rediscovering the path to spiritual success. The process of recovery has three stages, which we will consider in turn.

Abraham returns to the life of faith

The first stage is seen in Abraham's journey to Bethel. The significance of Bethel in the story is that it was the last place where Abraham had expressed his devotion to the Lord (v. 4). Here we have a picture of repentance in the Christian life. It was not sufficient for Abraham to return to the nearest location within the promised land, nor could he merely assume that he could start anew when he crossed the border. Instead he had to retrace his steps right back to where he went wrong.

The temptation is always there for a backsliding Christian to try to take shortcuts in repentance. When we backslide, we need to ask ourselves, 'What was the effect of my sin?' The effect reveals the seriousness of it. We don't discover the seriousness of our sins by comparing them with the sins of other people; instead we are to note what has happened to us because of our sin.

We can see this with Abraham's sins in Egypt. His request to Sarai that she pretend to be his sister was based on a half-truth (Gen. 20:12). We see the sin's seriousness through its effects: danger for Sarai, deceit, indifference, and other evil effects. When Abraham was confessing this sin, he would have had to dig to the root of why he committed it. And so do we. We should not treat sin lightly because we know it will be forgiven when we confess it. Instead, repentance has to be heart-work, otherwise it is just a sham.

In addition, the devil may try to tell the backsliding Christian that there is no hope: that he or she has sinned away the opportunity of knowing the Lord's blessings again. The devil's aim is to create despondency, perhaps with the intention of confusing the believer and making him or her think that despondency is part of repentance. Each Christian has to learn that repentance does not come about through the devil's assessment, but through listening to what God has to say about it. His word is that 'If we confess our sins, he is faithful and just to forgive us our sins and to cleanse us from all unrighteousness' (1 John 1:9). The

Lord's promises, and not the devil's twisting, are to be the focus when we repent of our sinful falls.

We see a marvellous example of the confidence that can exist in the heart of a penitent believer in the words of David in Psalm 51:12–13: 'Restore to me the joy of your salvation, and uphold me with a willing spirit. Then I will teach transgressors your ways, and sinners will return to you.' Then there is the promise that Jesus gave to Peter when he fell into sin: 'Simon, Simon, behold, Satan demanded to have you, that he might sift you like wheat, but I have prayed for you that your faith may not fail. And when you have turned again, strengthen your brothers' (Luke 22:31–32).

When penitent believers ignore the devil's attempts to distract them and his desire for shortcuts, they can have a profound experience of repentance in which they draw near to the Lord with a broken spirit and a contrite heart, and discover that he is full of mercy and willing to restore them freely and completely. Then they will sing with David in Psalm 103:10–12: 'He does not deal with us according to our sins, nor repay us according to our iniquities. For as high as the heavens are above the earth, so great is his steadfast love towards those who fear him; as far as the east is from the west, so far does he remove our transgressions from us.'

Abraham and Lot separate

The second stage in Abraham's recovery was to remove sources of tension that were potential causes of trouble. Shortly after he left Bethel, a problem arose within the family of Abraham due to inability to find enough pasture for their flocks. Here was a second test for Abraham. The first had been about how he would cope with famine, and he had failed that test. How would he cope with this new test?

The author informs his readers about a surprising aspect of the problem. Within the country, it was not possible for the servants of Abraham and Lot to live together, yet the Canaanites and the Perizzites could do so (vv. 5–7). Here we have a picture of a very common but sad reality. The disciples of Jesus, depicted by the family of Abraham, cannot live together in peace, yet the world, depicted by the people of Canaan, can do so. I suspect that Abraham realized that the quarrelling of the servants was removing any effective witness they could have for God in that area.

So what did Abraham do? Remember that God had given to him every inch of the land of Canaan, and there is no record that he gave even one inch to Lot. Yet Abraham willingly gave up his right to tell Lot where he was to go and instead allowed Lot to have the choice (vv. 8–9). In this response of Abraham's I think we can see several developing features of his spiritual outlook.

One feature that is exhibited here is Abraham's willingness to trust in the sovereign control of God. The patriarch realized that God's promises would not be fulfilled through human ingenuity that cut corners; instead they would be experienced as he displayed a godly attitude. This way of seeing things goes straight against worldly wisdom, which would have advised Abraham to put himself first. But Abraham had learned, through his descent into Egypt, that common sense is not always the best policy.

Here we see Abraham beginning to have victory over what seems to have been a defect in his character. We all have defects, and one that the biblical accounts indicate in Abraham was his determination to preserve himself at the expense of others, which he did twice, even with regard to his wife. It is a lot easier to deal with personal defects when we are in the path of obedience to God's will; it is impossible to deal with them when we are living in disobedience. Instead of preserving himself, Abraham here was willing to let Lot have the first choice.

Abraham's decision here points to another development in his character: the presence of humility. He could have said to Lot, 'Look here: I took you on this journey because you promised you would not cause any trouble. Why can't you control your servants?' Instead

Abraham, I suspect, would have said to himself, 'I wonder if it is my servants that are causing this problem? In case it is, I will take steps to prevent them defending my rights in a sinful way.' Whatever the reason, Abraham expressed a humble attitude. Here we have an example of the wise man's advice, 'A soft answer turns away wrath, but a harsh word stirs up anger' (Prov. 15:1).

A third feature seen here in Abraham as he returns to the path of spiritual success is his willingness to make tough decisions, decisions that included a certain amount of self-sacrifice. Abraham realized that he and Lot had to separate, which of course meant he had to lose fellowship with a person he loved. Sometimes the path of following God can take costly turns, and we find ourselves making decisions that are very hard. An example of this is when a minister gets a call away from a congregation he loves. The call of God, in that case, is to separate in order to continue on the path of spiritual success.

What about Lot? He, too, was being offered an opportunity to live on a path of spiritual success. Abraham gave him the choice of the land of Canaan. Peter tells us that Lot was a righteous man who was greatly upset by sinful practices (2 Peter 2:7). So what decision did Lot make? He decided to choose the fertile Jordan Valley (vv. 10–11).

I suspect the author is telling us that Lot chose a location where he would not have to depend upon the Lord. Moses says that the valley was 'like the land of Egypt', which means it would not have famines. From a natural point of view, it was ideal ground for a person with herds and flocks. We can imagine Lot saying to himself, 'I am glad I came here. I wonder how Abraham is getting on, trying to find water for his flocks.' It may have been harder for Abraham, yet he was on the path to spiritual success. In contrast, Lot was on the path to spiritual ruin. If we find ourselves in situations where we don't have to trust in the Lord regarding what he has given us, we are on a slippery slope. Moses tells us that eventually Lot ended up in Sodom, a wicked city. But his choice had blinded him and he could not see that he was in the wrong place.

We will see in later chapters some of the consequences for Lot of his choice. Briefly, he found himself involved in the wars and defeats of Sodom, he discovered that his children had absorbed the outlook of Sodom and even brought it into his own experience, and his wife became a permanent memorial to the judgement of God: some of the sad consequences of a selfish decision made by a righteous man.

Abraham receives assurance from God

Although Abraham had lost fellowship with his fellow-believer, he discovered that God could more than make up the loss for his servant. The Lord came to him and encouraged him with an expanded promise (vv. 14–17).

One detail to note from this promise is that Abraham lost nothing by his willingness to make a spiritual sacrifice. The Lord did not say to Abraham, 'Look in every direction apart from the east, which Lot has taken for himself.' Instead Abraham was told that he would have all that he could see, including the area that Lot had chosen for himself. It is impossible to lose out from serving the Lord. Jesus told his disciples in Mark 10:29–30: 'Truly, I say to you, there is no one who has left house or brothers or sisters or mother or father or children or lands, for my sake and for the gospel, who will not receive a hundredfold now in this time, houses and brothers and sisters and mothers and children and lands, with persecutions, and in the age to come eternal life.'

Furthermore, Abraham was encouraged by God to go wherever he wished in the promised land. We suggested in the previous chapter that his travelling in the promised land is a picture of Christians travelling in a spiritual sense through the range of blessings God has given them. Abraham, now that he has returned to the right path, discovers once again that he has full liberty to explore his inheritance. There are not any no-go areas in the land of spiritual blessing for those who return to the Lord.

We can recall that Moses earlier had pointed out that the Canaanites and Perizzites were still in the land. Outwardly they seemed more powerful than Abraham because they were more numerous than him. Yet contained in this command/invitation from the Lord is an implicit promise of divine protection. In the spiritual life, there are enemies intent on preventing Christians from discovering their God-given treasures, such as assurance, insight into God's great purpose, and aspects of salvation. Despite their weakness, they discover that their God enables them to overcome these opponents and explore their inheritance.

Moses closes this account by mentioning that Abraham did move to another location, the oaks of Mamre near Hebron (v. 18). There he continued the type of lifestyle he had before he went to Egypt, depicted by the tent (pilgrim travelling home to God) and altar (worshipper of God). He had rediscovered the path to spiritual success.

Fight the good fight (Gen. 14)

M oses gives his readers some historical details as he describes the next incident in the life of Abraham. The cities of the plain (Sodom, Gomorrah, Admah, Zeboiim and Zoar) were in bondage to an alliance of rulers from cities further to the east ('Amraphel king of Shinar, Arioch king of Ellasar, Chedorlaomer king of Elam, and Tidal king of Goiim', v. 1). This captivity lasted for twelve years before an opportunity arose for them to throw off their oppressors. They enjoyed their new freedom for a year before their enemies came on a military campaign to recover their lost territory. It was a successful campaign, as verses 5–7 reveal:

In the fourteenth year Chedorlaomer and the kings who were with him came and defeated the Rephaim in Ashteroth-karnaim, the Zuzim in Ham, the Emim in Shaveh-kiriathaim, and the Horites in their hill country of Seir as far as El-paran on the border of the wilderness. Then they turned back and came to En-mishpat (that is, Kadesh) and defeated all the country of the Amalekites, and also the Amorites who were dwelling in Hazazon-tamar.

In passing, we can note that Moses was informing the children of Israel, for whom he originally wrote Genesis, that the inhabitants of Canaan could be defeated, a rebuke to those Israelites who refused to enter the promised land because they were afraid of the size of the people who lived there.

Inevitably, the army from the east reached the cities of the plain and won a comprehensive victory over their former vassals (vv. 8–10). As was customary in those days, the victors took as booty all that belonged to their defeated foes, including captives who would become slaves. Among the captives and booty were Lot and his possessions, including his herds (v. 12). Interestingly, his wife is not mentioned, which suggests that he was not married at this time, and could indicate that he met his wife later in Sodom.

Are there lessons for us in what happened to Lot at this time?

Three lessons from Lot

First, it has often been pointed out that Lot was now living in Sodom. Moses does not tell us how many weeks or months it took for Lot to arrange this move. To begin with, he lived in his tent near Sodom (13:12), but now he was living in a house within the evil city. He had ceased to live a life separated from this evil community and was in danger of further adopting the outlook of the inhabitants. Here we have a picture of how compromises are made. Little by little, God's people adjust their outlook until eventually they are content to live where God's name is not honoured.

Second, for all we know, one of God's main reasons for allowing the invasion in his sovereign control of events was to rescue his child Lot from the culture of Sodom. The deliverance was certainly one reason for the incident; other reasons may have been connected to the wickedness of the society. It is very encouraging, or it should be, to know that the Lord does not leave his people in the snare of their own folly. He is prepared to use whatever it takes to deliver them from spiritual danger. Here we have an example of heaven's scales: it was better for Lot to lose his possessions than for him to keep on living in the sinful city. This is a reminder that God's deliverances may be very costly for backsliders.

Third, the question arises: Why did Lot put himself in a position in which he was likely to lose his freedom and possessions? Even if he had not known about the political situation when he made his choice to move to that area, he would have discovered the state of affairs very soon after. Further, it is also probable that he would have known something of the power of those eastern kings because they came from the part of the world he had left when he joined with Abraham. Perhaps Lot imagined that the defences of Sodom were sufficient to protect him from losing what he had gathered.

The answer to our question is that the presence of earthly wealth can blind us to the dangers connected to it. Obviously there is nothing wrong with becoming wealthier as a result of business prosperity or inheritance. Nevertheless, the pursuit of wealth for its own sake will definitely cause spiritual problems. Paul makes this clear in 1 Timothy 6:9–11:

But those who desire to be rich fall into temptation, into a snare, into many senseless and harmful desires that plunge people into ruin and destruction. For the love of money is a root of all kinds of evils. It is through this craving that some have wandered away from the faith and pierced themselves with many pangs. But as for you, O man of God, flee these things.

Lot had lost the ability to see things in a clear spiritual light. We can know that our hearts are blinded when we knowingly dismiss the dangers that are around us. Concern about spiritual enemies is a sign that we are seeing things clearly. We should not want to become like the believers mentioned in 2 Peter 1:9 who, because of wrong priorities, had become short-sighted (not seeing ahead to heaven) and had developed a bad memory (forgotten that they had been cleansed from their old sins). Lot says to us, 'Don't forget what happened to me!'

As we know, Moses' focus here is on Abraham, not on Lot. So what did this incident in the life of Lot mean for Abraham now that he had repented of his lack of faith expressed in going to Egypt and had resumed his life of devotion as demonstrated by his living in tents and building altars?

The experience of Abraham

Abraham was still in Mamre, the place he had gone to after his return to Bethel. There he had made friends with a local family composed of three brothers, Mamre, Aner and Eschol, who were probably the ruling family in the area of Hebron (v. 13). It may be that these men were only friendly pagans, but I don't think Abraham would have been so friendly with them if that was the case. He had been told by God to depart from paganism in Ur, and it is difficult to imagine that he would resume such contact in Canaan.

We are not told a great deal about this family, but we can deduce one point: they did not have any long-term objections to Abraham building an altar near them (13:18). Perhaps they did to begin with but, once Abraham told his story, they embraced his message of the true God and began to worship with him. Alternatively, given that Abraham was content to stay at Mamre, perhaps here he had found a family who had the same knowledge of God but given to them through the teaching of Melchizedek. The point I think Moses is making is that these men are an example of what God had promised to Abraham when he said he would be a source of spiritual blessing to others. Lot went down to Sodom and found himself without true friends, whereas Abraham lived as a pilgrim and found true friends who were willing to share his difficulties.

In the providence of God, one of Lot's servants managed to avoid capture by the enemy forces. He decided that the man to help the captives was Abraham (v. 13). What is striking about this man's search is that it was not difficult for him to find Abraham. Perhaps there had been some contact between Abraham and Lot and they had kept in touch after their separation. However, I think it is more likely that the servant, as he began his search, had only to ask people if they knew where Abraham was. They would have required information of his regular habits in order to identify him. The servant would have said, 'Abraham prays a lot, does not take part in pagan worship, but instead speaks about the true God and builds altars to him.' Immediately the people would have said to the servant, 'That man is in Mamre.' Maybe they also asked, 'Why do you want to see him?' The servant would have replied, 'His relative Lot, along with everyone else in Sodom, was captured by a strong army. I am going to tell Abraham because I know he will be able to do something about it.' If that was the scenario, the people may have laughed (what could Abraham do against such a great army?)—but the servant would have been right.

This possible state of affairs raises a question for us. If someone was looking for us, and had only several spiritual practices as identifying marks, would others in our community be able to direct the searcher to us? The seeker would say, 'The man I am looking for prays, speaks about Jesus and loves to go to church as often as possible. Have you seen him?' Such a person will stand out in the community.

The servant reached Abraham very quickly; we can work that out because the enemy forces had not travelled very far. When Abraham heard what had happened, he immediately resolved to rescue Lot (v. 14). On this occasion, the first response that springs from the man who lives in a tent and builds an altar to God is brotherly love for a fellow-believer in danger. Abraham need not have reacted in such a way. He could have responded by deducing that God was judging Lot for his worldliness and that therefore he should not interfere. Alternatively, he could have said that he and his men would be no match for the powerful kings who had captured Lot. But Abraham did neither. Instead he resolved to fight on behalf of his captured relative.

RESOLVING TO FIGHT

Here we have a picture of a common aspect of spiritual warfare: fighting on behalf of other believers who have so weakened themselves that they cannot fight for themselves. It is a reminder that we are part of an army. We can imagine a wounded soldier being easily captured by a group of enemy soldiers but being rescued by some of his fellow-soldiers. This happens often in the Christian life. It means that in the battle we don't merely watch out for ourselves, but we also keep an eye on our fellow-believers in case they are weakened. Usually the problem comes from the weapons of the enemy, but sometimes it is caused by their failure to protect themselves. Nevertheless, healthy soldiers cannot ignore those who have been wounded.

What are the weapons that healthy Christian soldiers should use? Abraham had to use physical weapons and tactics, although he no doubt made use of prayer as well. In the spiritual battle, prayer is essential. Paul includes it in his description of the Christian soldier in Ephesians 6 where he lists a spiritual counterpart for every piece of a Roman soldier's armour. The complement of the war cry of the advancing soldiers is prayer. Often, in ancient battles, it was the noise of the soldiers that frightened the enemy. It is certainly the case that nothing frightens the army of the kingdom of darkness so much as the sound of prayer coming from the Christian camp. The invading army here would have become aware of the advance of Abraham by the noise of his men, and the devil should be aware of our advance.

Another weapon that Abraham could have used as he pursued Lot was the promises of God. Where was Abraham as he chased after the enemy? He was in the territory the Lord had promised to give to him, and he was living in it as he should—in a tent (as a pilgrim) beside an altar (as a worshipper). The invading army had no authority from God to be there, but Abraham did, and therefore he was able to fight confident that the Lord would give him victory in the land of promise. It is the same with ourselves. If we live in the land of spiritual blessings, we will defeat the enemies of our souls because the almighty God is on our side. This is the argument of Paul in Ephesians 1:3. As believers we have all been blessed with all spiritual blessings (similar to how a new British citizen receives all the benefits of being part of Britain, even though he or she will be aware of only a small fraction at that moment), but in order to enjoy them we should anticipate our marvellous future, assess our inestimable riches and appreciate the immeasurable nature of God's great power, as Paul prays in Ephesians 1:18–19. We cannot have this enjoyment if we live in an equivalent of Sodom and are in spiritual bondage as a consequence. Abraham, who had been defeated in Egypt, knew that God would give him the victory in Canaan, which is what happened.

A third weapon is perseverance in rooting out the enemy. Abraham and his men ensured that the invading army was chased far enough away in order never to become a threat again (v. 15). They did not cease pursuing when the enemy began to run away; if they had done so, the enemy would have regrouped and returned another day. Instead, they had to weaken the enemy as much as possible. This has its equivalent in the Christian life. If I have a problem with a particular sin that is enhanced by certain books or television programmes, I will not defeat it if I merely stop reading the books or watching the programmes for a few weeks. Instead, I have to remove their influence completely by ceasing to use them, otherwise they will re-assert their influence. What is true individually is also true corporately. The church in Corinth was riddled with party spirit, each member aligning with a particular leader. There was only one way for the problem to be solved: each person had to cease doing it. If even just one person insisted on keeping his or her wrong attitude, the church in Corinth would continue to be disunited. The sin of favouritism had to be rooted out. Weakening of the enemy has to be done effectively in order for ongoing victory over it to take place.

Lot's situation would have looked ridiculous if Abraham, after he had defeated the enemy, then proceeded to argue needlessly with the brother he had rescued. Abraham could have remonstrated with him, pointing out the danger of his ways. Instead, at the close of this incident there occurs a sad return by Lot to the place of danger. Believers who fight in a spiritual sense for weakened brothers and sisters should not be surprised when they return immediately to a place near to where the problem began. The victory was Abraham's, not Lot's. Lot came away from this incident a rescued man, but not a repentant man. He may have concluded that Abraham was merely doing his duty as a relative. Whatever he deduced about the incident, Lot received no spiritual benefit. To be the recipient of a costly spiritual blessing without a spirit of repentance is a tragedy.

Blessed by Melchizedek

It is not clear whether this incident took place immediately after Abraham returned or a few days later when sufficient time had passed for an official ceremony to take place. The location is identified as the Valley of Shaveh (v. 17), which is near the site of the city of Jerusalem. Two different kings come to meet Abraham: Melchizedek descending from Salem with refreshments for Abraham and his men (v. 18), and the king ascending from Sodom with a suggested alliance (v. 21).

A lot of unnecessary speculation has focused on Melchizedek, with some suggesting that he was Shem the son of Noah and others suggesting that he was a pre-incarnate appearance of Christ (if he was, then Abraham would have been on his knees in worship). The reason for these suggestions is later biblical references which link the priesthood of Melchizedek with the Old Testament Messiah (Ps. 110) and with Jesus (Heb. 7). It is true that Melchizedek was a picture of Christ (who is both a king and a priest), yet his role was not merely figurative. He was a real historical person who ruled over a city where not only was the true God worshipped, but the political ruler led the worship himself. Abraham recognized the authority of Melchizedek, which suggests that they had met previously.

The presence of such a godly leader in Salem points to divine provision by God for his chosen agent, Abraham, in the promised land. Presumably the king-priest of Salem was able to instruct Abraham in the knowledge of the true God. It is likely that Melchizedek was in a line of individuals descended from Shem who had kept the faith despite the rapid departure from it that marked most of the other descendants of Noah. The existence of such a person is a powerful reminder that the Lord is able to continue his cause, no matter the extent of apostasy and evil that exists.

Melchizedek provided Abraham and his men with a meal made up of bread and wine. We should resist the suggestion that this provision depicts the Lord's Supper; these items were the normal food and drink of people at that time. Nevertheless, these items are symbolic because they were provided by God's representative for God's servant. They should have been a reminder to Abraham that his God would provide for all his needs.

Why did God arrange for Melchizedek to appear at this moment? His arrival must have been connected to Abraham's victory over the invaders. In addition, I would suggest that the Lord, whose timing is always perfect, knew that Abraham was about to face another fierce battle, a conflict with potentially serious consequences if he was defeated. This conflict was not with the invading armies who had been defeated; it was a temptation coming from the king of Sodom.

Melchizedek came not only with a meal for Abraham, but also with a reminder for him. The reminder concerned information about his God, who is described as 'God Most High, Possessor of heaven and earth' (v. 19). In other words, Abraham was told that God's resources would always be sufficient for all his future needs. He was reminded of the reality that Paul would later describe in this way: 'And my God will supply every need of yours according to his riches in glory in Christ Jesus' (Phil. 4:19). The priest of Salem and the apostle of the Gentiles join hands across the centuries and say to God's people that his grace will always be sufficient.

The reminder contains another important detail which we need to hear after a victory we have enjoyed. Melchizedek stressed that the reason for the victory was not Abraham's superior forces or cunning, although his forces may have been better trained and he did use the tactic of surprise when he attacked at night. Whatever the contribution of Abraham, all the glory had to be given to the Lord, which is why Melchizedek said, 'Blessed be God Most High, who has delivered your enemies into your hand!' (v. 20).

In response, Abraham gave Melchizedek a tithe, a tenth of the booty he had captured. This is the first mention of this practice in the Bible and reminds us that tithing was not begun as part of the Jewish ceremonial law. While it is possible that Abraham began the practice here by a voluntary donation, it is more likely that he had been instructed before, perhaps by Melchizedek himself, that tithing was an appropriate way to express gratitude to and dependence upon the Lord. And it still is, when possible.

The suggestion of the king of Sodom

The king of Sodom was probably concerned that Abraham would hold on to his captured booty. The people he brought back (v. 16) belonged to Abraham and he could have held on to them. The king realized that he needed the captives in order to protect his city; therefore he made the suggestion that Abraham keep the goods but return the people (v. 21).

Abraham's response shows that he had grasped the message of Melchizedek about the resources of God being sufficient for his people. Indeed, Abraham's words (v. 22) indicate that he performed a public act declaring that he was going to depend on the Lord and not on the forced generosity of a pagan king. This public declaration may have taken place when he gave his tithe to Melchizedek.

The king of Sodom may have imagined that Abraham would be a compromising backslider like his relative Lot, who was ready to receive all that Sodom could offer. Instead, he discovered that Abraham did not want anything from him. The patriarch was determined that no hint of concession regarding devotion to God would be found in him. Therefore he would not take even a thread (vv. 23–24). Separation to God covers little things as well as big things.

There is a parallel here between Abraham's response to the suggestion of the king of Sodom and Jesus' refusal to accept the offers of the devil during the period of temptation in the desert. Just as Jesus later refused to move an inch, so Abraham refused to take even a thread. In line with the custom that his friends had a right to their share, he allowed Aner, Eschol and Mamre their portion (v. 24). But he saw that it was better for him to refuse all that he could have taken legitimately, because he knew what had happened to Lot when he had accepted a place in Sodom.

So Abraham continues to make progress in the devotional life. He now knows how to fight for God, and, even more importantly, how to handle spiritual victories in his life.

The Lord enlarges his covenant (Gen. 15)

Often in the spiritual life, the reaction to a great triumph of faith is not increased confidence, but a loss of it. We have an example of such a loss here in Abraham. We might have imagined that after his great victory over the kings of the east Abraham would be strong in faith for all aspects of his religious life. Perhaps he was not apprehensive of these kings any more. Nevertheless he was very concerned that there was no sign of the fulfilment of a crucial detail in God's great promise to him. Several years had passed since Abraham had arrived in Canaan, yet there was no sign of the promised seed.

One of the intriguing features of this incident is the manner of dialogue between God and his servant. The first detail to note is that the Lord took the initiative in the interaction. He drew near to Abraham in a sovereign manner. The Lord was aware of the concerns of Abraham and in compassion he came with great delight to give further information to his loyal friend. This is how we should regard times of fellowship with God. It is not only the human participant who gets pleasure from times of communion between God and man.

Further, this delight of the Lord involved listening to what his servant had to say. God was already fully aware of Abraham's concerns and of the divine answer that would meet his need. Still today the Lord wants to hear the voice of his child, and often he delays his answer until the human request is made. We have very little awareness of the joy the Lord experiences when we pray. We tend to focus so much on ourselves that we fail to consider the thoughts of God.

Another detail to note in this interaction is the patience of God. He was willing to wait while Abraham specified his concerns. The Lord did not answer them all at once but responded to each in turn. This tells us that God wanted his friend Abraham to know in a clear way that the Lord was still committed to the promises he had made many years before. In a sense we can see the patience of God in the way he repeats promises and instructions throughout the Bible. He goes to great lengths to ensure that we understand who he is.

The description of God

The Lord informed Abraham that he had a divine shield and a great reward (v. 1). In other words, God said that he is the one who protects and provides for his people. These words reveal that Abraham was in a situation of permanent conflict in which he would be the recipient of divine supplies. It may be that Abraham pondered what had happened to Lot: how he had been easily captured and had lost all that he had when the invading kings defeated Sodom and its allies. Whether he did so or not, Abraham was reassured by God that such a defeat would not happen to him. Here is a divine promise to a faithful believer. This is the reward of grace.

When we apply this promise to ourselves, we need to ask this question: How often do I need God's protection? The answer is obvious: we need his protection all day long, every day, because we face spiritual enemies that are determined to destroy us. 'For we do not wrestle against flesh and blood, but against the rulers, against the authorities, against the cosmic powers over this present darkness, against the spiritual forces of evil in the heavenly places' (Eph. 6:12). We are not to imagine that it was any different for Abraham; he too had to deal with temptation and other forms of satanic assault. Yet the same promise that was given here to him is also given to us as long as we too are faithful to our calling.

Similarly, we should ask ourselves a question regarding God's resources: How much can God give us? The answer to this question is given in Philippians 4:19: 'And my God will supply every need of yours according to his riches in glory in Christ Jesus.'

It is important to note that when we speak of defence and reward here we are actually speaking about God. They don't refer to something apart from God. We could put it this way: a king could build a castle to defend his people, but the castle would be separate from him. That is not how we are to think of God. Instead, *he* is our castle. Similarly, a king could give out of his wealth to his needy subjects, but he himself would not be given with the gifts. But God is with the resources he gives. For example, the peace we receive is the peace of God; the joy we can know is the joy of God; the power we can experience is the power of God. Obviously God does not give us these blessings in their fullness at any given time because we could not cope with such an amount. Yet what is given to us is really God himself.

The question of descendants

The story informs us that Abraham was very concerned about the fact that he was childless. And according to the custom of the times, his heir would be his servant, Eliezer of Damascus (vv. 2–3). There seems to be a pause between what Abraham says in verse 2 and his next words in verse 3. Perhaps he wept in between his statements, or maybe he repeated himself in order to stress the great concern he had. In any case, the Lord assured Abraham that he would have a son who would be his heir (v. 4).

In addition, God gave to Abraham a sign in order to confirm his faith. He told Abraham to look at the stars of the sky and see in them a picture of his descendants (v. 5). Of course, it was not possible for Abraham to actually count the stars because he could not see most of them. Yet we can see how every night Abraham would have received assurance as he looked at the God-given signs in the heavens. The Lord gives signs because he knows we need memory aids, sources of comfort that will help us as we wait for his promises to be fulfilled. He has given us many signs. Baptism is a sign that sinners can be cleansed from their sins and join his people. The Lord's Supper is a sign that we can have fellowship with the crucified Christ who is now risen from the dead. Indeed, each Christian is a sign that God is at work in the lives of sinners. We have been given clear signs of God's presence with us as we wait for him to fulfil his promises in the new heavens and new earth.

The Lord did something else for Abraham at this time in response to Abraham's correct use of the God-given sign of the stars. Abraham responded to the sign in faith and the Lord re-confirmed to Abraham the standing he had before God: 'And he believed the LORD, and he counted it to him as righteousness' (v. 6). We are not to imagine that this was the moment when Abraham was justified. Rather he had been justified when he first believed in God. But here Abraham was in need of assurance of his standing with God, and it was given to him because he made a spiritual use of the sign. It is similar with us, if we make the biblical response of faith to the signs we have. When we use the Lord's Supper as we should as a means of recalling the substitution of Jesus for us at Calvary, or as an anticipation of his return in the future, or as a place where we receive heavenly graces, we will discover that God strengthens our assurance and we become convinced of our standing with him.

The question of the land

Again God took the initiative in the conversation and reminded Abraham that he had promised him the land of Canaan as his possession (v. 7). Despite having received a sign shortly beforehand, Abraham asked for another one (v. 8). His request was not necessarily an indication of unbelief; it could have been prompted by him realizing that God-given signs were a means of discovering more about God. We have to remember that Abraham did not have a Bible and he was dependent on ways such as visions and signs in order to find out what God was like and what he would do. And Abraham did learn more important truths about God as a result of asking this second question.

The Lord told Abraham to arrange three animals and two birds as a sacrifice (v. 9). Abraham cut the animals in two and placed them in such a way that there was a gap down the middle (v. 10). Then he was to stand guard over the sacrifices, protecting them from birds of prey (v. 11). At sunset he fell asleep and had an unusual dream or vision, and it was then that he was given further details by God concerning his descendants and himself (vv. 12–16).

Commentators regard this occasion as the time when the Lord made Abraham a prophet. The phraseology 'the word of the Lord came' is usually used in the Old Testament of messages that were given by God to prophets. We can see that something similar is the case here because the Lord gave to Abraham several predictions concerning his descendants. This new information was not only for Abraham's benefit, but also for subsequent generations, giving them a framework by which they could understand what happened to them. So what would they have discovered from this prophecy?

First, they discovered that it was God's plan that their ancestors should be in Egypt for four hundred years (v. 13). This long period of time was due to the sinful practices of the people in the land. Despite the presence of godly rulers such as Melchizedek and devout people like Abraham, the sinful practices of the inhabitants would get worse. Eventually their culture would have to be destroyed. Often new readers to the Bible are surprised at the divine command given to Joshua to slay the inhabitants of Canaan, imagining it to be an act of barbarism that reduces the God of the Bible to the level of pagan idols. A little knowledge of Canaanite practices will quickly dispel that notion. Among these practices were child sacrifice. What were the alternatives facing the children of Israel? They would either have to tolerate or destroy such practices, and God wanted them removed from his land. Sometimes a society becomes so evil that the only remedy is to remove it completely.

There were other reasons for the captivity of the children of Israel. One is connected to the previous comment: it was probably better for Abraham's descendants to be in trouble in Egypt than to be tempted by the false religions of Canaan. This principle is often true at an individual level: God allows problems and suffering to happen in order that we will not fall into sinful practices.

A third reason for the time in Egypt was to teach the children of Israel not to trust in the great powers of the earth. Initially, they were well treated in Egypt, but eventually they became slaves. The descendants of those rescued by Joseph persecuted his descendants. Instead of seeing human powers as their defenders, the Israelites would have to depend on the supernatural power of God to protect them.

Fourth, from the experience of Egypt they would also learn that God judges sinful practices. Although Egypt persisted in enslaving the Israelites, the Egyptians were eventually punished by God in a very costly way. Power that is abused will eventually be judged by God, but he will not do it until the time is right. Often the difficulty we have is connected to the length of the delay. We cannot tell when God will arise, but we will see it when it happens. Revenge was not to be part of the outlook of Israel.

Fifth, the Lord revealed to Abraham another important principle: that times of testing are enriching times. Perhaps the Israelites would have wondered how they could possibly become a great nation, given that they were enslaved in poverty. Yet they were assured that, when the Lord arose to deliver them, they would leave Egypt with great riches (v. 14).

We may ask ourselves what this experience has to do with us. Initially it seems to be irrelevant for our daily living in the modern world. Yet there is a very important lesson, which is that the framework by which we make sense of our world must be the revealed will of God. When we realize this, we will also discover that this word to Abraham becomes part of God's word for us in making sense of life in a sinful world.

In the midst of these dire predictions, Abraham received another word of assurance. Remember that he was almost on his own in a strange land in which there were many enemies. Perhaps he feared sudden assassination. Whatever his thoughts may have been, the Lord assured him that he would defend him throughout a long life (be his shield) and give him a peaceful end (from his resources) when he would be united with the family of God in heaven (v. 15).

Does God not do the same for us? Often he sends words of heavenly assurance to comfort us in the midst of our troubles. Great and precious promises are given to the suffering and tempted people of God. Whatever the pathway, they can know the protection and the provision of the Lord in many unexpected ways. We are not like Abraham, needing visions and unusual visits to bolster our comfort. We have the Word of God, and Paul reminds us that the Old Testament, including this story about Abraham, is given for our spiritual benefit: 'For whatever was written in former days was written for our instruction, that through endurance and through the encouragement of the Scriptures we might have hope' (Rom. 15:4).

Before we leave this incident, we should note the significance of the Lord, under the symbols of smoking firepot and flaming torch, passing between the pieces of the slain animals (v. 17). In Abraham's time, two people making a covenant would walk through that path as a sign of commitment to their promises, indicating by so doing that if one of them showed disloyalty he could be torn in pieces like the animals. Yet in this instance, the Lord alone walked through the pieces—for at least two reasons. First, the Lord knew that Abraham in himself, despite his good intentions, did not have the power or the wisdom to bring about the promises of God. Second, the Lord indicated to Abraham a very solemn reality: God would be finished if he did not keep his promises to Abraham.

Chapter 6

What greater evidence could the Lord give of his determination to bless Abraham with a seed and an inheritance! In fact, there is only one greater Sign, and that was given when the One who spoke that night with Abraham became the curse on the cross. But the meaning is the same: Jesus died to ensure that the seed of Abraham would have an inheritance.

Abraham and Hagar (Gen. 16)

A braham had been tested in several ways since he arrived in the promised land. First, he had been tested by famine; he had failed that test because he chose to find help in Egypt rather than remain in Canaan and depend on God. Second, he had been tested by family ties when the land became too small to cater for his herds and those of his nephew Lot; Abraham passed that test by allowing Lot to go where he wanted. Third, he had been tested by the prospect of reward from the pagan king of Sodom after the invading kings had been defeated; but Abraham passed that test by refusing the king's offer. Each of these tests had come shortly after times of spiritual triumph. In Genesis 15 Abraham had gone through a mountain-top experience when God enlarged for his servant the content of his covenant. So he should have anticipated another test soon. And it came—through his wife Sarai, when she suggested to him a plan for fulfilling God's promise.

There are different ways of reading the account of this incident. Wonderfully, it reveals much about human character and about divine grace. It is the story of a woman (Sarai) who was desperate for God's promise to her husband to be fulfilled. It is also a story about how Abraham was not spiritually alert to the dangers inherent in her suggestion. And it is the account of how the Lord cared for a person who was insignificant in the eyes of the world (Hagar), who had been harshly treated, who had been abandoned by those she knew best, but who discovered grace in an unlikely way.

The advice of Sarai

Abraham and Sarai had been a decade in Canaan, but there was still no sign of the promised heir. They had been assured by God that the heir would be their child and not a servant in their household. Sarai had obviously been thinking about the matter and her conclusion is given in verse 2: 'Behold now, the LORD has prevented me from bearing children. Go in to my servant; it may be that I shall obtain children by her.' It is possible to read her words as blaming God for the situation, although I suspect she is merely acknowledging his providence in her life. She had attempted to read providence and used her deduction as to how God's promise should be understood. Yet instead of reading providence through God's word, she had read God's word through providence, and there is a big difference between the two responses.

Her error was connected to two factors: her own inability and the presence of a solution. Perhaps she imagined that God's promise was not to be taken literally when he said that they would have a son. The fact that he had not given them one was proof of this. Before their very eyes was the answer, providentially provided by God and in agreement with the practice of the times. It was regarded as appropriate behaviour for a wife to use her female slaves in order to obtain children by her husband. We can see this practice in action in the family of Jacob when his wives, Leah and Rachel, both use their female slaves in this way. So Sarai imagined that she had found an answer to a real dilemma, and like most people who imagine such a discovery, she was quick to pass on her insight.

What was the cause of Sarai's suggestion? I don't think it came initially from unbelief. Instead it came from impatience with God. She wanted the Lord to operate according to her timetable; after all, she was getting old. A correct response to the Lord's delay in fulfilling his promises is one of the most difficult achievements in the Christian life, especially when it concerns an issue or a person precious to us. Of course, we know that the

Lord was testing Sarai and that eventually he would fulfil his word to her and Abraham. But it is easier to remind another person to hold on in faith than to maintain that attitude ourselves.

Are there any ways we can help ourselves develop this outlook of patience? One obvious way is to continue in prayer and leave the working out of the answer to God. This spiritual activity is not escapism; it is an expression of confidence in God's love, wisdom and power. Another way is to recall how we have been dealt with personally. A common burden among disciples is unconverted relatives. Many people prayed for me for years before I was converted, and I suspect that none of them could have imagined the means by which the Lord would answer their prayers. The fact that God did answer those prayers eventually is an example of his choosing the best way, arranging all the circumstances and persons involved, and bringing the answer in his own time.

There are other matters about which we pray, but for which we have not yet received an answer. Perhaps we want a certain legitimate position or possession for ourselves or for others. We have prayed about it, and so far God has not given it. Yet we realize that it is possible to manipulate circumstances to increase our chances of getting it. We can argue that God has placed these circumstances in our way in order that we might use them to attain our goal. The danger about this type of trying to get an answer to our prayers is that God does not stop us proceeding with our intentions. Sarai received no indication from heaven that she should not go through with her plan. Yet we should know that divine silence is not necessarily a sign of approval.

An obvious conclusion from Sarai's proposal is that shortcuts are never a method of fulfilling God's will. There is a sense in which the devil's temptation to Adam and Eve concerning the way to obtain knowledge was a shortcut. He tried the same policy with Jesus when tempting him in the desert, offering him highest success if he forsook

God's path for an easier and shorter way. We should be suspicious of shortcuts to spiritual success.

Sarai quickly realized that she had made a big mistake. Her slave Hagar no longer showed her any respect, and she immediately blamed Abraham (vv. 4–5). Our initial response is to gasp at her accusation because, after all, she had suggested the plan. She discovered that her impatience with God's will and her suggested solution had merely shown up a weakness in her husband's outlook. Sarai learned by hard experience that Abraham could not be trusted to act the right way at all times. There is a word to husbands here: What do you do when your wife makes a wrong suggestion? Abraham did what Adam did in the Garden of Eden: he went along with his wife's suggestion instead of reminding her that her idea was inappropriate.

Abraham also revealed another inappropriate response when he failed to take responsibility for Hagar and her infant (v. 6). Instead of ensuring that compassion be given, he allowed cruelty to be shown towards them. At no stage did he intervene in the harsh treatment and say that mercy should be shown. Sarai's response was based on jealousy, but Abraham's response was based on indifference and a failure to ensure that she behaved in a godly way. But there was One who cared for Hagar, and his eye was on her as she was expelled from the safety of her home (presumably she had been with Abraham and Sarai for the decade since they had returned from Egypt).

What all this tells us is that God uses sinners in his plans. We are not here to point the finger at Abraham and Sarai; they are pictures to help us see where we come short.

The angel and Hagar

Moses then introduces us to this mysterious figure called 'the angel of the LORD' (v. 7). This is the first of many references to him in the Bible. We can see from his words in verse 10 that he was not a mere angel, because an angel could not bring to pass the promise of a great number of descendants; only God can perform such a feat. The fact that this angel was divine is also revealed in the response of Hagar in verse 13, when she says that she has 'seen' God. This divine appearance is called a 'theophany' and it is generally suggested that the person who appeared in this manner was the Son of God. In other words, the person who spoke to Hagar was the same divine person who would later be called Jesus.

The first point to note is that the Son of God knew where Hagar was and he came to her in her time of need. He was prepared to do what neither Abraham nor Sarai was prepared to do. This reveals to us the great compassion and kindness of God, his willingness to descend into a location where a poor woman was alone. Was this not a foretaste of what he would later do with regard to the woman of Sychar when he met her by the well near her village (John 4)?

The second detail to observe is that the Son of God called her by her name (v. 8). No doubt her initial response was to wonder how a stranger knew who she was. When a person calls you by name, it is usually a sign of friendship, of interest in us. Friendless Hagar discovered that she had a friend who stuck closer than a brother.

Third, the Son of God addressed Hagar regarding her position in life when he called her the 'servant of Sarai' (v. 8). Sarai may have thrown Hagar out, but that was not how he saw her position. Sarai's action was wrong and here the angel of the Lord ignored it in the sense that it had not changed anything in the relationship between Hagar and Sarai. I suspect that Hagar was here being reminded of her entrance into the world of grace. Ten years previously, she had been a pagan in Egypt. Through the providence of God, she had been brought into the community in which his name was known. In that community she had discovered the true God and become one of his people. Although she was still a bondslave, she had known for ten years that it was better to be with the people of God than to dwell in the tents of sin.

Fourth, the Son of God asked Hagar where she had come from and where she was going. These questions were not displays of ignorance; they were designed to point out to Hagar where she had gone wrong. In other words, the Saviour was leading his child to confess her fault. Hagar seemed to realize this because she confessed that Sarai, despite having cast her out, was still her mistress. Although Sarai had been harsh, Hagar had also sinned by despising her mistress. Hagar was being called by her Lord to deal with her personal sin and return to her mistress and acknowledge that she was a slave. She was being called by God to repent and return to live with his people.

Fifth, the Lord gave to penitent Hagar a wonderful promise that dealt with her current fears. Although she was a slave, her son would become a mighty warrior (vv. 11–12). The Lord also revealed to Hagar that he had listened to her prayers, even though up till then his providence suggested otherwise.

This was a remarkable experience that was given to Hagar. During the decade she had been with Abraham's family, she would have heard him speak often of the gracious God who had revealed himself in Ur and many times since then, giving promises and other aspects of divine help. Perhaps Hagar had wondered if she would ever experience such blessings from her master's God. Well, she did. She received assurance that the Lord watched over her, listened to her and was taking care of her future. It would have been straightforward to return and confess her faults to Sarai, knowing that God was with her and helping her.

Sixth, Hagar gave God a name. She called him the 'God who sees me' (v. 13, margin). This means that from then on she and God had a secret to share, a matter about which she could have fellowship with him. She had had a personal encounter with the God of grace and she would never forget that she had met with him. This encounter would give her great confidence for whatever the future would bring her way.

Seventh, she had a message for Abraham and Sarai. The message was that God has comforting words for sinners, that he takes care of them and provides for them. I wonder what Sarai thought when she saw Hagar walking back into their camp. This was an unusual providence for her to think about, but hopefully she noted that her God was also the God of her servant.

Sign of the covenant (Gen. 17)

Twenty-four years have passed since the Lord called Abraham to set off to the promised land, which is a reminder that God can take a long time to fulfil his promises. Between twelve and thirteen years have passed since Hagar returned to Abraham's camp after meeting with the God who had been looking after her during her flight and then intervened in her life in a dramatic way. Although the biblical record is silent regarding any further revelations given to Abraham during those years, there may have been such. It is wrong to assume that God was silent throughout that period if we cannot give any proof. The best response to those years is not to focus on them but instead to regard the recorded incidents as the ones that God wants us to reflect on. So the author wants us to consider the next incident which he describes: the occasion when the Lord gave to his servant Abraham a covenant sign by which he and his company were distinguished from all other groups.

Promise amplified

On previous occasions, God had given promises to Abraham. Some of these had been fulfilled, such as the promise on his conversion that he would be led by God to a special country. Others had not yet been fulfilled, such as the promise that he would have a son and that his descendants would inherit the land of Canaan. Now Abraham was to receive more information about God's plans for him.

Before he enlarged on his commitment, the Lord did two things: first, he revealed a detail about himself and, second, he specified a requirement, a necessary response, from Abraham.

How did God describe himself to his ageing servant? The Lord said that he was 'God Almighty' (El Shaddai) and was so permanently (v. 1). We can see the emphasis on permanence when God said 'I am'. In other words, he always is who he says he is. The name 'God' (El) itself means 'power', so 'Shaddai' probably points to his infinite resources that are conveyed through his power. We can note that we often need divine strength in order to experience what God can give (see Eph. 3:16–19).

By getting Abraham to focus on particular attributes—those of omnipotence and infinite resources—the Lord was instructing him about making a very basic but important response to God: Abraham should consider the divine attribute(s) that was/were most suitable for his needs to be met and God's promises fulfilled. The Lord, as it were, invited Abraham to consider what his God was capable of doing. In saying that he is almighty, he was reminding Abraham that divine power fulfils divine promises. He had promised Abraham a son and there was no possible way for Abraham to work out how God would keep this promise. The only fact he knew was that a miracle was required, an action beyond the power of a creature to bring about. But the God who made all things out of nothing could give him a son.

In the light of the revelation of himself, the Lord now made a requirement of his servant: 'Walk before me, and be blameless' (v. 1). This requirement was of a twofold nature: the Lord desired company with Abraham and consecration from Abraham. Walking with another person is a picture of fellowship, of companionship. We expect friends to be loyal to one another and not to engage in actions detrimental to one another. The Lord demanded of his friend Abraham that he live in a manner suitable to his privileged position; in other words, the only way by which a sinner could be a friend of the Lord's was through ongoing consecration. If Abraham failed to be loyal, God would regard the covenant as broken. So the patriarch had to walk with God, as the Lord said, so 'that I may make my covenant between me and you, and may multiply you greatly' (v. 2).

It may be helpful for us to note what others have said about God's requirement here that Abraham should be blameless. C. H. Spurgeon, in a sermon on this chapter, explained the meaning of 'blameless' as 'sincerity':

However, the word 'perfect' ... bears commonly the meaning of 'upright', or 'sincere'—'walk before me, and be thou sincere'. No double dealing must the Christian man have, no playing fast and loose with God or man; no hypocritical professions, or false principles. He must be as transparent as glass; he must be a man in whom there is no guile, a man who has cast aside deceit in every shape, who hates it, and loathes it, and walks before God, who sees all things with absolute sincerity, earnestly desiring in all things, both great and small, to commend himself to the conscience of others as in the sight of the Most High. Brethren, here is the model of the consecrated life.[1]

Robert Candlish, in his *Studies in Genesis*, explains 'blameless' in this way:

To walk before God, is to walk or live as in his sight, and under his special inspection: to realise, at all times, his presence and his providence; to feel his open and unslumbering eye ever upon us. To walk thus before God is impossible, if there be not redeeming love on his part, apprehended by faith on our part; and to be perfect, guileless, and upright, in thus walking before God, is the great duty of the believer. He alone can discharge that duty. Others do not like to retain God in their knowledge; they have comfort only when all serious thought of God is got rid of, and put aside; and so they hide themselves from God amid secular vanities or sacred formalities. Their walk is not, and cannot be, in good faith, a walk before God, or with God, under his eye and subject to his control. But as to his own people—why should they not walk before God? Why should they not, with entire openness and uprightness, so walk? Why should they shrink from so close a fellowship with God as such a walk implies? Having peace with him, and making it their single aim to be like him—why should they not be perfect in such a walk?[2]

Abraham's response to this divine pronouncement was an act of worship: he fell on his face (v. 3). As his servant lay prostrate on the ground, the Lord proceeded to outline his plans, in which Abraham was going to be a major player. The covenant had two parts. First, it contained the promise that Abraham would be the father of many mighty nations, not just of the Jews and the Arabs, as is commonly said (vv. 4–6). Second, specific mention was made of Abraham's descendants who would live in the land of Canaan, that the Lord would be their God. As a sign of his commitment to his purpose, the Lord now gave Abram the new name Abraham, which means 'father of many nations'.

There is an important lesson for us here regarding discovering or understanding the will of the Lord: God reveals his mind to those who engage in worship of him. Would God have continued speaking if Abraham had remained standing and self-important? Obviously, a physical position need not indicate the state of one's heart, and it is possible for hypocrites to engage in external worship. But the principle is true: usually God speaks to those who are devoted to him. McCheyne said on one occasion that a person is what he is before God. The secret place of devotion is where we discover who we are as well as who God is and what his plans are. Many a person understands the Bible's promises on his or her knees far better than in a classroom.

What is the significance of a new name? Usually in the Bible a name points to a purpose or a desire on the part of those who gave it. God often gave new names to people. For example, he renamed Jacob as Israel, which means 'prince with God', after Jacob had spent the night wrestling with the Lord and prevailed. Abram seems to have been the patriarch's name before he met the Lord in Ur. His new name, Abraham, would be a permanent reminder to him that the Lord was working on his behalf.

Our minds probably go to the incident when Jesus renamed Simon with the name Peter, which means 'rock'. At that time, Simon was the opposite of a rock: unreliable and unpredictable. But Jesus was indicating to him that he would be changed by divine power, and this did take place. Eventually, unstable Simon developed into trustworthy Peter because of the life-changing power of Jesus Christ.

Another person who changed his name was Saul of Tarsus. While it is possible that he had more than one name from childhood (the Hebrew name Saul and the Greek name Paul), it is interesting that Luke, in the Book of Acts, begins to call Saul by the name Paul after the probable conversion of the Roman governor of Cyprus, Sergius Paulus (Acts 13:9). It is possible that Paul chose his new name because the Lord had kept his promise and had enabled him to witness effectively to rulers (Acts 9:15).

Those who believe in Jesus are given many new names, and each of them has great significance. For example, slaves of sin become sons of God, unclean sinners become saints, undisciplined sinners become disciples, and enemies of God become his friends. We should think often on the new names that God has given us because each of these names contains great blessings.

In his letters to the seven churches, Jesus uses the imagery of a new name to stress that his followers will yet inherit the promised blessings of glory. In Revelation 2:17, in the letter to the church in Pergamum, Jesus promises: 'To the one who conquers I will give some of the hidden manna, and I will give him a white stone, with *a new name* written on the stone that no one knows except the one who receives it' (emphasis added). At the very least, this illustration points to the fact that one aspect of the heavenly experience will involve secrets shared by each believer with Jesus. And in his letter to the church in Philadelphia Jesus says: 'The one who conquers, I will make him a pillar in the temple of my God. Never shall he go out of it, and I will write on him the name of my God, and the name of the city of my God, the new Jerusalem, which comes down from my God out of heaven, and my own new name' (Rev. 3:12). The possession of these names points to divine ownership (the name of a master was often stamped on a slave in one way or another) and service.

Returning to Abraham, after he had received his new name, he was never to call himself by his old name, no matter how silly his new name might have sounded to others. His neighbours and others in the vicinity would all have known what his new name meant, and no doubt some of them dismissed his explanation of it as fantasy. We too can be tempted to live more in line with our old ways than with what God requires of us, especially if we know that others will mock us for what we say about faith in Christ. But if Jesus has given us a new identity, we should confess it to others and not be ashamed of it.

What did God mean when he promised Abraham that his descendants would have the land of Canaan for an everlasting possession (v. 8)? It cannot have a literal meaning because we know that earthly territory will cease on the Day of Judgement. Even if the Jews were converted tomorrow and lived in their country for a thousand years, it would still not be an eternal possession. Since the promise is not literal, it must be symbolic. Under the imagery of a particular country the Lord was promising Abraham that his descendants would have an eternal inheritance.

Similarly, who were the descendants of Abraham who would inherit the promised land? If we take it literally, we have a problem because we know that many Israelites, including devout ones such as Ezekiel and Daniel, did not live in Canaan. Further, we also know that many of his physical descendants were wicked people. Yet God said to Abraham that in the future all his seed would live in the same place where they would be blessed by God. Moses, when he recorded this incident as he composed the Book of Genesis, already knew that many of Abraham's literal descendants were not believers in God. Yet he recorded this covenant promise because he knew that the fulfilment of it would occur in

Abraham's spiritual seed (God's true people), as Paul explains in Galatians 3:29: 'And if you are Christ's, then you are Abraham's offspring, heirs according to promise.'

Sign of assurance

The Lord then informed Abraham that he had to engage in a specific duty: to circumcise all males within his community, beginning with those currently alive, and performing it on all future males when they were eight days old (vv. 9–14). What was the purpose of this ritual? One answer is that it identified those who were connected to the promise of God and those who were not connected. Some object to this idea because other nations of the time practised this ritual. Yet their ritual pointed to purposes different from that of Abraham. The crucial point is not that they were circumcised, but that they had been circumcised by Abraham or one of his descendants. We may not be impressed by that argument since the outward effect was the same, no matter how the individual had been circumcised. Yet it was important that the ritual be accompanied by an explanation of its meaning. This is why we do not perform any of our two covenant signs (baptism and the Lord's Supper) without a suitable sermon based on the Word of God.

This sign identified the recipients as belonging to the community within which the promises of God would be ordinarily fulfilled. It was always possible for God to bring the revelation of himself to people outside the covenant community, as he did with individuals such as Job and his friends. Yet this was probably the moment when the Lord set up an organized community composed of those who worshipped him. In a sense, it is the origin of the church from an earthly point of view.

Partners together

The Lord informed Abraham that his wife Sarai would also get a new name—Sarah (v. 15), although both old and new names had the same meaning: 'princess'. The Lord seemed to be stressing two points with this new name. First, since he had given the name, Sarah would have a God-given reminder of his promise; and second, he was confirming to Abraham that the future royalty of their extensive seed would come through her (v. 16; a princess gives birth to royalty). The Lord wanted them as a couple to embrace his future for them, which is a powerful message for Christian couples today. They should anticipate together the glory that is yet to come and bring up their families in the light of it.

Abraham's response was to laugh (v. 17). Since the Lord did not rebuke him for this, we must assume that it was a laughter generated by faith and expressing delight in God's covenant promises. It is significant that Abraham laughed when he was told that Sarah would share the blessing, which speaks volumes about his love for her. This too is a challenge to us, whether as couples or simply as believers: do we express our delight in the blessings the Lord gives to others whom we love?

Naturally Abraham wanted Ishmael to share in the blessing. So he prayed earnestly that Ishmael might have a prominent place in God's purposes (v. 18). Some interpret this request as indicating that Abraham wanted Ishmael to be the heir rather than Isaac. I think rather it is the prayer of a devoted father who wants his child to do something great for God. Perhaps it is similar to the request made by Salome that her sons might have a prominent place alongside Jesus on his throne (Matt. 20:21). But God said no to Abraham. This did not mean that Abraham could not pray for the salvation of Ishmael, which I am sure he did every day. Rather Abraham was forbidden by God to pray that Ishmael might be outstanding in God's purposes. That place belonged to Isaac and his descendants. Nevertheless, Ishmael would be blessed in his place in society as an answer to Abraham's prayers (v. 20). And Isaiah 60:7 contains a promise that the descendants of Ishmael (Nebaioth was his son) would yet join the people of God.

Obedience

The next verses highlight one important detail: instant obedience. Abraham, Ishmael and the other males were all circumcised that day (v. 23). No doubt some of them wondered what was going on, but obviously the explanation of Abraham persuaded them to comply.

We live in a society in which most things can be classified as instant, especially since the development of the Internet. But the most important 'instant' of all is the necessity of obeying God's commandments immediately. This should be our response to all his requirements. If we do so, we will be like Abraham as he determined to walk before God in a blameless way.

NOTES

1   C. H. Spurgeon, *The Treasury of the Old Testament*, Volume 1 (London: Marshall, Morgan & Scott, 1951), pp. 87–88.
2   Robert S. Candlish, *Studies in Genesis* (Edinburgh: A & C Black, 1868), p. 266.

Sarah's laugh (Gen. 18:1–15)

Noneof us knows what a day will bring. Generally, life continues from day to day without much change, yet occasionally a very significant moment arrives. Often these days can be anticipated: a wedding is looked forward to by all involved, a birthday celebration is a time of family togetherness. Sometimes we can be looking forward to an important event when an unexpected incident arises. Perhaps a person about to be married receives an unforeseen offer of new employment, and adjustments have to be made to plans that seemed straightforward.

Abraham was waiting for God to fulfil his promise that he would have a son. Given the ages of Abraham and Sarah, the day of fulfilment would be one of great amazement at the ability of God as well as at his faithfulness to his promises. We can imagine Abraham wondering how it would all work out. Yet there was a problem because the narrative in Genesis 18 reveals that Sarah, despite her new God-given name, did not believe that the Lord could perform his promise. This situation had developed in her spiritual life, and it is an outlook that is both very common and very serious. It is common to find lack of faith, and it is serious because the Bible reveals that, although God is omnipotent, he does not respond favourably to unbelief concerning his promises. The situation was made worse because Sarah had been given specific promises about what God would do for her.

Here God drew near to Abraham with a twofold mission. First, he came to deal with the issue of unbelief, and, second, he came to involve Abraham in his plans. Perhaps Abraham had realized that Sarah had a problem with unbelief and therefore he had been praying about it. Such a response would have been the obvious one for a devoted husband to make. Observation of her unbelief should have made him more prayerful about her spiritual state. While we cannot prove that this was what happened, we can yet see an important lesson for ourselves concerning how we should respond to spiritual defects in our spouses or other family members who express unbelief. Abraham could not sort out Sarah's problem; no amount of reminding her of God's promises seemed to be working. Abraham did have God's word on the matter, but he did not have God's power to bring about a change. Therefore he prayed for God to sort out the issue. When we see a similar problem we have to pray for God's power to be displayed, and eventually he will come and do something about it. So this incident helps us prepare for sudden visits from God.

It is not clear when Abraham realized that one of his visitors was divine. His addressing one of the travellers as 'my lord' (v. 3) was a common form of courtesy, similar to how we might address a person as 'sir' or 'madam'. From the details given in the account it looks as if the moment may have been when the Visitor referred to Abraham's wife not only by name, but by her new God-given name. The use of the name 'Sarah' must have made Abraham sit up and take notice (v. 9). Further, the prediction given by the Visitor, that he would return in a year's time and arrange the birth of their baby son (v. 10), must have been noticed by Abraham. In addition, the Visitor's knowledge of Sarah's response of laughter must have told Abraham that the Visitor was divine. These three details would have prepared Abraham for his time of intercession with God that is described from verse 16. In this chapter, however, I want us to think about the Lord's mission on behalf of Sarah.

First, we can see that God not only comes suddenly, but he can often appear in disguise, as it were. Here he appeared as a man, and the two angels with him also appeared as men. Other people would not have known that the Lord had appeared to Abraham. All his neighbours would have seen was three strangers being given a meal. It would have been very difficult for Abraham to say that the Lord had visited him. This arrangement was the Lord's doing. Several reasons can be suggested for this divine method, some more satisfying than others.

One suggestion is that since God is invisible he has to hide who he is whenever he takes on a temporary human form. In other words, because God will always be greater than the method he chooses to use, it is inevitable that he will be hiding something of himself when he appears. No doubt that is true, yet it does not explain why the Lord appeared in this way to Abraham. God could have appeared in a form that displayed his power: he could have performed public miracles or displayed his authority over the creation. It is clear that the Lord could have appeared in a manner that caused the entire community to realize that he was present. But he did not do so.

Another suggestion is that he appeared in this manner in order to have a private meeting with Abraham. It is unlikely that neighbours or members of Abraham's community would interrupt his social responsibility to give a meal to strangers. No doubt God did want to have a personal meeting with his friend Abraham. But he could have appeared to Abraham in a dream or vision, as he did at other times. So while there is truth in this suggestion of a personal visit, I think there are more likely explanations.

It seems to me that the Lord appeared in this way to Abraham in order to prevent his boasting. When the Lord gives special privileges, he usually does so in a manner that makes it difficult for the recipient to boast about it. Paul received a thorn in the flesh to stop him becoming proud of his visit to the third heaven (2 Cor. 12:7); Jacob received a permanent limp after his wrestling with God at Peniel (Gen. 32:24–32). Imagine a neighbour saying to Abraham, 'Who were the men you fed yesterday?' If Abraham replied, 'They were the Lord and two of his angels', the neighbour would conclude that Abraham was either joking or losing his sense of reality.

This kind of experience can often be ours. We can have an encounter with God in a church service and be deeply affected by it. However, when we mention it to another worshipper he or she says that nothing unusual happened in the service and gives the impression that we imagined it. We had a secret meeting with God, but the very circumstances of it prevent us boasting about it. When that happens, we should thank God. It is better to be given a blessing in a manner that prevents our boasting than to be given one in a way that allows pride to develop.

Second, we should notice the time when the Lord appeared. He arrived during the time of day when Abraham would not be engaged in other activities. In hot climates, outside work was not done at noon because the heat was unbearable. It was, therefore, a suitable time for God to receive full attention from his servant. For all we know, this was the time of day when Abraham had his private devotions. What is important to note is that the Lord came at a time that was suitable for Abraham as well as for God. If the Lord was arranging a visit to us, would he be able to find a time when he could meet with us face to face, without interruption?

Many years ago, I heard a fellow-Christian say, 'Beware the barrenness of a busy life!' We live in a society in which busyness is a virtue but also a major cause of stress. Those who make themselves busy every moment of the day will soon find that they cannot cope. That happens at a natural level, but it also takes place at the spiritual level. If Abraham had worked through the heat of the day, he would have collapsed. If we cannot find space for God to meet with us, we are too busy and we will miss out on spiritual blessings.

God is very accommodating. He adjusted his schedule to fit in with Abraham's daily programme. And he will do so for us as well, as long as we have space for such a meeting to take place.

Third, we should note the response of Abraham. Throughout the hours of the day he was in charge of the affairs of his compound. He was the master who gave out the orders, and we see this in the way he urged Sarah to prepare a meal for the travellers (v. 6). Yet how different was his demeanour before the Lord! Instead of being the master, Abraham became the servant: he expressed humility by bowing down to the earth; he expressed eagerness by showing haste; he expressed honour by sacrificially giving a suitable animal. Once the meal was ready, he stood beside them, indicating his availability to do more if required.

Sometimes we wonder why God does not speak to us. Perhaps we should ask ourselves: What is my attitude when I engage in personal devotions? Are they a routine duty, with no sense of anticipation? Or am I doing them in order to avoid receiving divine judgement, with no sense of delight in God and his promises? There are many inappropriate ways of having personal devotions. Is it likely that God is going to speak to us comfortably or consolingly if we are not marked by the features seen here in the response of Abraham? Absence of humility, eagerness, willingness to sacrifice and availability for service will prevent us hearing the voice of God.

Fourth, we should consider how the Lord brought Sarah to face up to her unbelief. His question to Abraham as to her location is not an indication of divine ignorance. Instead God was telling Abraham about one purpose of the visit, which was to specify that the promise of a son would be fulfilled in a year's time. Since Sarah was listening in to the conversation, we would expect that increased information would have encouraged her faith. Yet it did not. Instead she reacted to the divine promise in a manner that was close to contempt (v. 12). The reason for her response was that she judged the situation by her inability and with the assumption that God always works according to fixed rules necessitated by human helplessness.

In noticing these aspects of her response, we are not regarding them as stones we can throw at Sarah. Instead we have to take our place beside her and confess that we are guilty of similar sins. Many listen to the gospel offer—which describes a supernatural activity of God, a salvation that cannot be provided by anyone else—and assume that somehow or other they are too sinful for God to change them. Such an attitude is the equivalent of Sarah's laughter. Others are aware of their past failures and deduce that, despite many biblical promises to the contrary, these sins mean they can never again experience a profound relationship with God. Again, such an attitude is the equivalent of Sarah's laughter.

How did the Lord react to Sarah? He asked Abraham why she laughed (v. 13). It may be that God was adapting himself to the social customs of the time in which a visitor would speak to a wife via her husband. But I don't think this was what the Lord was doing because he shortly afterwards spoke directly to Sarah. Instead I suspect that the Lord was pointing out to Abraham that this failure in Sarah's spirituality was connected to her husband. Perhaps Abraham had been remiss in stressing the faithfulness of God to her; or perhaps he had failed to remind her of the many ways God had provided supernatural help for them (such as protecting her when she was in Pharaoh's harem, or enabling Abraham to deliver Lot from a powerful army). Is this not implied in the question that God asks: 'Is anything too hard for the LORD?' (v. 14). It does seem as if Sarah had been denied faith-building exercises, and the Lord held her husband responsible.

This responsibility still rests with those who serve God. Sometimes men make the remedy harder than it is. In the realm of physical exercise, it seems that taking a regular walk is as effective as going to a gym for most people. A simple activity can produce the results we need. Likewise, a husband may imagine that he has to come up with an innovative scheme that will transform the home, whereas the remedy lies in simple things such as directing conversation in the home towards the things of God, or suggesting that prayer be made for a particular matter. Little things, even things that may be regarded as mundane everyday activities, are usually the answer. (We note in passing that this responsibility does not mean that the wife can never take the initiative, but it does mean that the husband cannot abrogate his role.)

Thankfully, this state of affairs did not cause the Lord to divert from his determination to fulfil his sovereign plan to bless them. In the midst of this family confusion he affirmed that he would keep his promise. At one level, this divine resolve is a clear reminder that human sin and failure cannot hinder God's purpose, and that is very encouraging when we recall the awfulness of the sins our society practises. Yet at another level, we see here the loving patience and persistence of God towards and with his children. The clearest example of this is the way in which the Lord Jesus responded to his disciples during the three years he spent with them. No other leader would have shown such loyalty and determination to bless followers as Jesus did day after day. We should take great encouragement from this divine response to Sarah's laugh.

Nevertheless, the repetition of the divine intention on this occasion did not deliver Sarah from her unbelief. She attempted to hide her sin (v. 15), which we know was a futile action in the presence of God. The reason for her wrong response was fear of God. Now, it is always important to have a right fear of God, an attitude of reverence and respect for him because of his perfections. But true reverence takes account of the fact that he is a gracious God. We can see here that Sarah's fear of God did not have this essential feature. Instead her wrong fear led her to try to impress on God that she was not guilty of her sin, that she would not have succumbed to such a wrong response as to laugh at God's promises. Her words are the verbal equivalents of the fig leaves that Adam and Eve wore after they had sinned against God. Instead of hiding the fact that they had sinned, the leaves only highlighted that they were guilty. Similarly, Sarah's denial did not hide her sin; it only revealed that she was guilty of wrongdoing.

When we try to behave in a similar manner towards the Lord, we will receive in our souls the same abrupt reply that Sarah received from him. He said to her, 'No, but you did laugh' (v. 15). This situation is very like the one in which David found himself when Nathan rebuked him for his sin with Bathsheba by saying, 'You are the man!' (2. Sam. 12:7). It is important for us to remind ourselves that the Lord will always be straight when pointing out our sins to us.

The reason why the Lord did this for Sarah was to bring her to repentance, and that is why he does the same for us. This is how we put ourselves back into the right path, as it were (of course, we recognize afterwards that the restoration was all the Lord's doing). We come to our spiritual senses and confess our sins to the Lord. In Sarah's case her repentance opened the door for her to experience the grace of God's fulfilled promise: 'By faith Sarah herself received power to conceive, even when she was past the age, since she considered him faithful who had promised' (Heb. 11:11). Although she had been in a state of unbelief, her gracious God came down to where she was, brought her to see her sin, and led her back into the life of faith.

It is intriguing to note that not every detail in Sarah's response is condemned by Scripture. Thousands of years later, the Apostle Peter was writing his second letter and one of the topics with which he dealt was women's adornment. He said that women should not concentrate on outward features such as hairstyles and clothes, but on 'the hidden person of the heart with the imperishable beauty of a gentle and quiet spirit, which in God's sight is very precious' (1 Peter 3:4). Peter chose an example, and surprisingly he selected this incident in Genesis when Sarah referred to Abraham with great respect by calling him 'my lord'. So Peter noticed that Sarah displayed good traits even when she was expressing unbelief at a supernatural promise concerning an activity that had never happened before. When we add to Peter's opinion the underlying fact that the Holy Spirit guided him as he wrote, we can see that even God the Spirit highlighted this feature in Sarah. The obvious lesson from this is that we should not allow our fellow-believers' weak points, even their sins, to hide their good points from us.

The intercession of Abraham (Gen. 18:16–33)

We noticed in the previous chapter that the three visitors, one of whom was the Lord himself, had come to see Abraham for two reasons. One reason concerned the spiritual unbelief of Sarah concerning the promise of God that she would have a son in her old age. The Lord requires that each of his people exercise faith as he fulfils his promises, and his loving confrontation of Sarah led her to go through that experience with a strong faith in God (as the author of Hebrews writes at 11:11 of his book).

The second reason for the divine visit concerned the necessity of divine judgement on a wicked city. Sodom was notorious for its wickedness, and not only for immoral practices. The prophet Ezekiel details other sins of Sodom: 'Behold, this was the guilt of your sister Sodom: she and her daughters had pride, excess of food, and prosperous ease, but did not aid the poor and needy' (Ezek. 16:49). Despite its sins, the Lord had given Sodom gracious warnings.

One of these warnings involved Abraham when he rescued those from Sodom who had been captured by the invading army from the east; the king and residents of Sodom had observed the help God gave to his servant Abraham and were also present when Abraham acknowledged that help by paying tithes to Melchizedek. The other warning was connected to the presence of Lot in their town. While he made a mistake in going there, Peter says that Lot was 'greatly distressed by the sensual conduct of the wicked (for as that righteous man lived among them day after day, he was tormenting his righteous soul over their lawless deeds that he saw and heard)' (2 Peter 2:7–8). The people in Sodom observed a man in their midst who was living a righteous life. So it cannot be said that they had not been warned about their sinful lives and were not aware that others worshipped the true God.

Before we look at some details of this incident involving Abraham, we should remind ourselves of two other references to Sodom: words uttered by the Lord Jesus himself. He told his disciples on one occasion: 'And if anyone will not receive you or listen to your words, shake off the dust from your feet when you leave that house or town. Truly, I say to you, it will be more bearable on the day of judgement for the land of Sodom and Gomorrah than for that town' (Matt. 10:14–15). Every true preacher is aware of that awful reality when he preaches the gospel. He knows that those who reject his message will have greater judgement on the final day than the judgement that will be given to Sodom.

Later, Jesus pronounced judgement on several cities in which he had ministered. Concerning Capernaum, he said: 'And you, Capernaum, will you be exalted to heaven? You will be brought down to Hades. For if the mighty works done in you had been done in Sodom, it would have remained until this day. But I tell you that it will be more tolerable on the day of judgement for the land of Sodom than for you' (Matt. 11:23–24). Capernaum had actually done what the inhabitants of Sodom would not have done: Capernaum had ignored the mighty works of Jesus, a response which Jesus reveals would not have occurred in Sodom. He indicates that the Sodomites would have responded in such a way that would have prevented the temporal judgement they experienced.

There is another key detail to note about the people of Sodom. Not only did they have a terrible judgement in the past, but they are waiting for an even worse judgement in the future. The fact that others will be judged more severely than them will not mitigate the experience of the people of Sodom in a lost eternity. Imagine these people today as they wait for this awful future encounter with Jesus, the Judge of all!

Having said that, we must remind ourselves, as we have done

previously with theophanies, that the person visiting Abraham here was none other than the Son of God before he became incarnate. So we have an insight into the outlook of Jesus concerning the fate of the inhabitants of Sodom, an outlook that he revealed to his friend Abraham.

The burden on the heart of God the Judge

As the visitors and Abraham began their farewells, the Lord, probably to Abraham's great surprise, turned to him and revealed the second reason for the visit: 'Then the LORD said, "Because the outcry against Sodom and Gomorrah is great and their sin is very grave, I will go down to see whether they have done altogether according to the outcry that has come to me. And if not, I will know"' (vv. 20–21).

We are not to make invalid deductions from these words. It is possible to read them in such a way as to suggest the Lord was ignorant of what was going on in Sodom. That was not the case. Instead we have here another example of how the Lord condescends to the capabilities of his creatures. We need to realize that God does this continually, whatever the situation. Even in heaven, where he is worshipped by the mighty and intelligent angels, the Lord reveals himself according to their capacity. The angels are creatures and as such are limited in their understanding. True, they have more understanding than us at present, but it is still impossible for them to know anything about God unless he condescends to reveal it to them in line with their capability.

The Lord is going to act as Judge in connection with Sodom. In fact, he is in the process of sitting in court. The trial is underway, and some witnesses have been heard. Their testimony is very serious: the Lord describes it as a great outcry and very grave sin. The 'outcry' may have been the cries of distress that were made by the people around Sodom who suffered because of its outrageous sins. Perhaps there is a similarity here with the event described in Job 1 and 2, when the angels report to God about their activities: their testimony of Sodom is that its inhabitants are guilty of great sin. Their evidence—whether the cries of distress of those afflicted by Sodom or the observation of ministering spirits commissioned to take care of Lot—is taken seriously by God the Judge.

This divine assessment of Sodom carries a strong message to our modern world. It is a reminder to nations and peoples that they cannot sin with impunity: there will be divine judgement. The Lord does not wait until the final day before he judges the world. Of course, the judgement on that day will be the ultimate one, but many judgements will have taken place before then. The judgements that happen before the final day involve temporal troubles sent in response to great ungodliness. This reality is seen repeatedly throughout the Bible, particularly in the messages of the prophets. One clear example of such divine judgement on nations is detailed in Amos 1 and 2, but many such divine messages were sent to the other ancient nations, such as Assyria, Babylon and Egypt. One thing is certain: the cries of injustice that are screamed from the earth today are heard in heaven, and God will bring judgement on the perpetrators.

A further accommodation that God makes in his role as Judge is to visit the scene of the crime. He did this previously with regard to the Tower of Babel (Gen. 11:1–9). Usually our judges do not do this because sufficient evidence is brought to the courtroom. It was common in ancient times for the judge to see as much evidence as possible because he alone decided the verdict. There was no jury to decide for him. So, in addition to hearing what witnesses had to say about a particular place or group of people, the judge would visit the place himself. No doubt, on occasion he would have to go to the situation in disguise because if the offenders knew he was coming they could easily hide their sins and create a pretence. In the case of Sodom, God came disguised as a man in order to see for himself the evidence that had been presented before the heavenly court.

Sometimes those who bear heavy responsibilities need others with whom to share their concerns. They don't share their concerns because they don't know what to do, but because they have valued friends who can empathize with them. Here was the Son of God describing his activities to his friend Abraham. We know this was not the last time the Son of God looked for empathy: in Gethsemane, when he was anticipating the divine judgement of the cross, he asked his three closest disciples to watch with him. If they had shown as much interest as Abraham did, they would not have fallen asleep.

Isaiah 59:16 describes the Lord's attitude to oppression: 'He saw that there was no man, and wondered that there was no one to intercede [for the oppressed]; then his own arm brought him salvation, and his righteousness upheld him.' It is probably true that very few were interceding for Sodom—perhaps just Lot and the household of Abraham. Even fewer would have been interceding for the victims of Sodom; and the Lord noticed it, and came down to deal with it.

Three reasons for sharing the burden

As he was about to leave, the Lord turned to the two angels and said to them that he did not want to hide his plans from Abraham (vv. 16–19). This means that God wanted his friend to have the same knowledge as the angels had: they knew why they were there. But the Lord wanted to tell Abraham himself, in private fellowship.

The basic reason given by the Lord for sharing the burden was that he had made great promises to Abraham. These promises included the revelation that through his descendants would come the means of universal blessing (the salvation that would be accomplished later by the speaker when he became a man, bore the wrath of God on the cross, was raised from the dead and exalted as Ruler of all). The basic qualification for sharing with God is to be a recipient of divine promises.

The second reason for sharing the burden was connected to Abraham's responsibility to teach his 'children' (plural, v. 19, so it refers to more than just Isaac) and his household to imitate God in the performance of righteousness and justice. The information that Abraham was to pass on was not based on the standards of human justice, no matter how elevated some of them might be. Instead he was to communicate the justice of God, but before he could do so he had to understand divine justice himself. Therefore God explained his justice to Abraham, and he was then responsible for instructing his family concerning it; they in turn would be responsible for passing these divine concepts on to their descendants. After all, the Dead Sea is a permanent reminder that the Lord judges wicked societies. Going back to Abraham, we can see that his enjoyment of the promises was dependent on the fulfilment of his responsibility to instruct his community about the ways of God.

The third reason for sharing the burden was linked to the special relationship between God and Abraham. Translations differ in expressing the bond in verse 19; some suggest it is connected to election ('I have chosen him'), while others suggest that it is an expression of intimacy ('I know him'). The latter seems the best option to me. Between God and Abraham there existed a precious loving relationship, perhaps the deepest there has been between a sinful human and God. Even if we cannot attain to the degree of Abraham's intimacy, we can still have an intimate relationship with the Lord.

The type of people with whom the Lord shares his burden are marked by these three features: they are recipients of God's promises, they live according to the righteous demands of God and teach them to others, and they get to know God intimately by spending time with him. Feature one is the stimulus, feature two is the condition, and feature three is the reward of a devout life. All three are the qualifications for legitimate intercessors.

The intercession of Abraham

The Lord and the two angels started on their journey (v. 22). It looked as if they would have to pass Abraham as they went, but he showed no sign of letting them leave. Instead he drew near to the Lord and asked a question that was troubling him: 'Will you indeed sweep away the righteous with the wicked?' (v. 23). Abraham was troubled by the possibility of the righteous experiencing divine judgement along with the wicked. He made the best response to such a concern: he brought it to the Lord.

Abraham realized that a court case was going on and therefore he appealed to the Lord in his role as Judge when he asked, 'Shall not the Judge of all the earth do what is just?' (v. 25). I suspect that Abraham was concerned about the reaction others would have if the Lord destroyed those who were loyal to him. In any case, he suggested that the presence of fifty righteous people should cause the Lord not to judge the city, and the Lord agreed to the request.

Abraham had doubts about the number of righteous there and eventually he reduced the figure to ten, but he received the same assurance from God: if there were ten righteous people, the city would be spared. As Matthew Henry observed, God 'did not leave off granting till Abraham left off asking'.[1] We are not told why Abraham stopped at ten. Perhaps he counted Lot and his wife and assumed that their children were married to righteous people. Maybe he sensed the energy of intercession fading from his soul. The fact is that there was only one righteous person in Sodom, and that was Lot.

What characteristics did Abraham display in his prayer of intercession? Several features can be identified from his prayer.

First, intercessory prayer must be based on a communication from God. The prayer of Abraham was a response to the information God gave him about Sodom. With regard to ourselves, we have a far greater divine communication—the Bible—and our prayers must be according to its teaching. It enables us to pray according to God's revealed will.

Second, intercessory prayer must be an expression of confidence in

God. Abraham was confident that the Lord would act justly and not destroy the righteous on this occasion, as otherwise it would give the impression that Lot and his family were unrighteous. This does not mean that righteous people never suffer during a time of judgement. Rather, the justice of God would ensure that his cause was not identified wrongly in his court. Nevertheless, Abraham's prayer was very bold because it was an attempt to influence the Judge. Yet that is what intercessory prayer is: an attempt to change the revealed will of God concerning a situation. For example, we know that our own society is under divine judgement, and we know that is the case because God has specified in his Word what will happen to such societies. Yet God does not require his people to sit back and wait for the judgement to fall, which is what will happen if they do not stir themselves to pray. God's revealed will says that his praying people can prevent temporal judgements from coming. Therefore, they can pray earnestly about the matter.

Third, intercessory prayer must be expressed by one who is consecrated to God. Abraham revealed his dedication in at least two ways. For example, he thought very little of himself—he was 'but dust and ashes' (v. 27). Although he had been given a new name indicating a prominent place in God's purposes, Abraham was still a humble man. Humility is essential to consecration.

Further, Abraham was sensitive to the possibility that he was intruding into areas into which he should not go, and he was afraid that such intrusion would make the Lord angry. I don't know if Abraham had seen others who had so behaved, but we know from the Bible that sometimes people can step too far into divine secrets; the friends of Job did so and were rebuked by God. The Bible indicates that sometimes even consecrated believers can step over the line; recall how the Lord attempted to slay Moses because he failed to circumcise his son (Exod. 4:24). It is a sign of consecration to be humble in demeanour and careful in one's boldness in the presence of God.

Fourth, intercessory prayer is concerned about those who are under the threat of divine judgement. Abraham did not only pray for the safety of Lot and his family, he also requested that the city be spared. He had realized a feature of the heart of God that the prophet Jonah failed to appreciate fully: that God is willing to show compassion to inhabitants of wicked cities, whether Nineveh or Sodom. Abraham knew that the Lord does not take delight in the death of the wicked and therefore he prayed fervently for them.

We are told then that Abraham went home, and the Lord 'went his way' (v. 33). I wonder what expression was on his face. Centuries later, that same Lord, now incarnate as Jesus Christ, would look over the wicked city of Jerusalem and weep (Luke 19:41). I cannot say what look was on his face as he made his way to Sodom, but I know what Andrew Bonar thought: 'I think that the shower of fire and brimstone was wet with the tears of God as it fell; for God has "no pleasure in the death of him that dieth".'[2] I suspect he was right.

NOTES

1   Matthew Henry, *Commentary*, on Gen. 18:23–33.
2   Andrew A. Bonar, *Diary and Life* (Edinburgh: Banner of Truth, 1984 [repr.]), p. 511.

Lot loses the lot (Gen. 19)

T he story is told that Oliver Cromwell ordered the artist who was commissioned to paint his portrait to do so, 'warts and all'. In other words, Cromwell, because he was a devout man, wanted posterity to have an accurate likeness of him. No doubt he learned to think in this way by noting biblical descriptions of the characters in the Bible. Frankness and honesty stand out in these accounts and the whole picture of their lives is given. Sometimes the biographical description is marked by great exploits and we admire the person who performed them; at other times, the story is marked by horrid and disgusting details. The story of Lot, Abraham's nephew, narrated in Genesis 19 falls into the latter category.

Yet we know that the story of Lot is also a story of personal tragedy. Although it includes disturbing details, the Bible makes clear that Lot was a pious man. Peter, when referring to the incident detailed in Genesis 19, informs his readers that God 'rescued righteous Lot, greatly distressed by the sensual conduct of the wicked (for as that righteous man lived among them day after day, he was tormenting his righteous soul over their lawless deeds that he saw and heard)' (2 Peter 2:7–8).

Robert Candlish summarizes what Peter meant about Lot:

That was his security; he retained his spiritual discernment, his spiritual state. He loved not them that hated the Lord; he had no sympathy with their ungodliness. He did not learn to palliate or excuse, either their unholy opinions or their unlawful deeds—to call them by smooth names, affect a soft and serene charity, and hope the best even of the world lying in wickedness. He was vexed—he vexed himself. The English word here is too weak by far. He was wearied, worn out, worn down, by the impieties with which the lawless were conversant. They were an intolerable burden to him. Thus the Lord knew how to deliver him, by keeping alive in his soul, amid abounding iniquity, an undiminished zeal for truth and righteousness, and an uncompromising hatred of all evil.[1]

Lot, as we can see, was not guilty of the sins into which David sadly fell—adultery and murder. So how did he find himself in such a difficult situation?

Before exploring the answer to this question, we must focus on Lot's spiritual state. As the quotation from Peter indicates, Lot was a godly man. It is certain that he had come to the knowledge of God through what had taken place in the life of his uncle, Abraham. Therefore, there was information that Lot would have known and believed. The most important detail concerned the promise of worldwide salvation through the descendants of Abraham. While it is not possible to say how much Lot knew, it is likely that with Abraham he would have recognized that the Messiah would come and deliver his people. I think it is safe to say that Lot's hopes of eternal blessing were linked to his faith in the promised Messiah.

Although he would have shared this understanding of God with Abraham, there are two details which he did not share. The first concerns the place where Lot chose to live. Lot must have deduced that God had limited the location of spiritual blessing to the family of Abraham. Yet Lot chose to move away from that influence and went to live in Sodom, and he persevered in staying there even after he was rescued by his uncle from those who had captured Sodom.

The second detail concerns his wife. While it is possible that Lot was married before he chose to live in Sodom, it is more likely that he found his wife there. His method of choosing a wife was so different from that of Abraham, who would later insist that the wife of his son Isaac was not to be taken from the local tribes but instead from his family back in Haran (Gen. 24). While the negative influence of Lot's wife may have been a factor in Abraham's outlook, it is more likely that Abraham's attitude was based on the necessity of having a wife who acknowledged the true God.

We can now proceed to examine the state of affairs in Lot's life when the two angels arrived in Sodom. In passing we should not imagine that angelic visitations are rare events. Job 1 and 2 indicate that it is a regular activity of angels to come down to earth on missions about which they report back to the heavenly courtroom. Paul reminded the Corinthians that angels were present in their church services, and he referred several times to angelic ministry in his life.

Lot the citizen

When the two angels entered the town they observed Lot sitting in the gate (v. 1). This location was a privileged place and indicates that Lot had become a councillor of the city (his position is later acknowledged in a dismissive manner by the crowd in v. 9). We are not told in what way he attained this position. No doubt his wealth marked him out as an important man, one suitable for such a role. Perhaps he took the position in order to try to change the awful behaviour of the citizens.

In addition to being a politician, Lot was also a courteous man (vv. 2–3). It was customary in the Middle East to offer hospitality to strangers and Lot was no exception to this rule. He should have been surprised at the initial response of the strangers when they refused his invitation. Perhaps they were testing him to see if he would persevere with his words of welcome; if it was a test, Lot passed it because he did persuade them to accept his hospitality. Yet I suspect that the refusal was more than a test: it revealed a reluctance to stay in his home. While Lot did not know that the visitors were angels, the reader does and is meant to observe that the inhabitants of heaven did not want to stay in the home of a believer on earth, which suggests that there was something wrong with that believer's home.

Regarding the provision of hospitality, no mention is made of Lot's wife, which is in marked contrast with the behaviour of Sarah when the visitors came to Abraham's tent (Gen. 18). Of course, the description in verse 3 may be shorthand for saying that both Lot and his wife were involved.

In any case, the author soon reveals that all was not well with Lot (vv. 4–11). Sodom was well known for its immorality and its inhabitants were determined to practise their sin and physically abuse the two visitors. In response, Lot was prepared to allow his daughters to be raped in order to be spared the embarrassment connected to disgraced hospitality (vv. 6–8).

It is important to note Lot's way of thinking: instead of being godly, it was at the level of the thinking of the inhabitants of Sodom. It does not seem to have crossed Lot's mind to ask God for help. A willingness to ask for divine aid is a sure sign of healthy spirituality. An awareness of sin in others is not always such a sign because such knowledge may come from previous instruction. Present dependence on God, however, is always an indication that the individual is conscious that he or she is in God's presence and can be a recipient of his help.

At that moment the angels revealed who they were and rescued Lot from physical assault by striking the men of the city with blindness (vv. 10–11). We should note that this act of supernatural judgement did not stop the inhabitants from attempting to continue with their intentions. There is an important lesson for us here as well: judgements, even personal ones, on people and communities do not in themselves bring people to repentance. There are many acts of divine judgement happening at this time— wars, famines, financial crises—and there is no sign of national repentance. Instead people continue practising the sins in which they engaged before the particular troubles came.

In verse 12 we have an insight into the attitude of angels as they are about to administer divine judgement. They informed Lot of their mission and urged him to bring his relatives out of the town. Lot realized that things were serious and told his relatives to flee, but his words fell on deaf ears. It is not clear whether Lot had four daughters, two of whom were married, or whether he had only two daughters who were about to be married. In any case, his two sons-in-law, whether married or about to be married, thought he was jesting. Is there a lesson for us in their response to Lot's warning? While we cannot say if Lot had failed to warn them previously, we can say that if he had not done so regularly, he could not have expected to be taken seriously when he began suddenly to do so. People have to see how our knowledge affects us before they will take our words seriously. It is hard to tell people about the destruction of a place if all they usually see is how eager we are to live in it with them.

Lot escapes

When morning dawned, the angels told Lot to leave the city and take his wife and daughters with him, otherwise he would be caught up in the judgement (v. 15). Strangely he was reluctant to go (v. 16), a reminder of how quickly we can forget acts of divine judgement (in his case, the blinding of the men of Sodom). Thankfully, the Lord was faithful to him and showed him mercy by instructing the angels to take Lot and his family out of the town. Verse 29 informs us that one of the reasons for Lot's deliverance was the prayer of Abraham: 'So it was that, when God destroyed the cities of the valley, God remembered Abraham and sent Lot out of the midst of the overthrow when he overthrew the cities in which Lot had lived.' This is encouraging because we know that Abraham did not specifically mention Lot by name when interceding for the city. But the Lord read the heart of Abraham and answered according to his longing and not according to his arithmetic.

The angels instructed Lot to go as far away as possible from the place of judgement (v. 17). Lot did not think he could reach the hills before being overtaken by the judgement, so he asked if he could go to another city instead, which was granted to him (vv. 18–22).

The moment Lot reached Zoar the judgement fell (vv. 23–25). What were the men of Sodom doing at that moment? Jesus says they were engaged in ordinary activities: 'Likewise, just as it was in the days of Lot—they were eating and drinking, buying and selling, planting and building, but on the day when Lot went out from Sodom, fire and sulphur rained from heaven and destroyed them all—so will it be on the day when the Son of Man is revealed' (Luke 17:28–30).

But not all who had been taken out of Sodom reached the safety of Zoar: Lot's wife looked back (v. 26). This does not mean that she glanced around; instead I suspect she stopped and looked back for a while and was overwhelmed by the burning sulphur and covered in it. Why did she do this? Because, although she had been taken out of Sodom, Sodom had not been taken out of her. Jesus refers to her as well in the passage cited above from Luke's Gospel: 'Remember Lot's wife' (Luke 17:32). He indicates what was wrong with her: 'On that day, let the one who is on the housetop, with his goods in the house, not come down to take them away, and likewise let the one who is in the field not turn back' (v. 31). She was worried about her possessions, and could not keep her eyes off them even when they were on fire. And she perished. Although delivered from the city by the hand of an angel, she never made it to the heavenly city.

Lot: the further descent

Moses gives further details about what happened to Lot (vv. 30–38). Tricked by his daughters, he became the ancestor of two tribes—Moab and Ammon—that were to be hostile enemies of Israel for centuries. What a legacy for a believer to leave! And it had all begun when he looked covetously on the plain of Sodom and decided to go and live there.

A question that should be asked is: Why did he not go and live with Abraham? If he had done so, this terrible pair of incidents and their consequences would not have occurred. Perhaps it was because of embarrassment that he had made mistakes, or maybe he found it hard to look in the eye a relative who had put God first. In any case, we leave Lot here. He had chosen to live in a place that had run out of time as far as God's judgement was concerned. The other inhabitants did not know that was the state of affairs, but he as a believer should have known that it was possible and have lived in the light of that possibility. The same is true for us: we don't know if our society is about to receive great judgement, but we should reckon it a possibility and live in such a way that shows we are not part of it.

Fortunately, Lot is in heaven, and if we go there at the end of our days we will see him made perfect in holiness, enjoying the glory of God and sharing the resurrection victory of Christ. He is an example of the wonder of the mercy of God. It is not for us to throw stones at Lot; instead we should ask God to keep us from similar spiritual mistakes and from making a mess of our lives.

And we will see the men of Sodom as well. Despite their great sins, we will see them receive less punishment on the Day of Judgement than that given to those who rejected Christ: 'And you, Capernaum, will you be exalted to heaven? You will be brought down to Hades. For if the mighty works done in you had been done in Sodom, it would have remained until this day. But I tell you that it will be more tolerable on the day of judgement for the land of Sodom than for you' (Matt. 11:23–24).

NOTES

1 Candlish, *Studies in Genesis*, pp. 314–315.

Same old sins (Gen. 20)

braham moved from Mamre (18:1) and headed south, eventually reaching the Philistine territory of Gerar. From one perspective, he seemed to be following God's command to walk through the land that had been promised to him (12:7). Yet we know that appearances can be deceptive.

The point at which Abraham made this move to forbidden territory is surprising. We have seen that he had recently enjoyed a profound experience of fellowship with God. Since he had been a participant in such communion and had received great promises, we would expect him to have continued in a state of spiritual devotion until Isaac was born. Yet Abraham did not do so.

Further, Abraham had just witnessed what had happened to Lot because of his venture into an unapproved location. Lot had moved to Sodom and, while he himself had escaped, he had lost everything in the divine judgement that fell on the city. Surely Abraham would have said to himself, 'I must be careful where I go in case something similar happens to me.' Yet he did not take the warning.

In addition to these recent happenings, Abraham had another reason for not going to Gerar. Years before, he had gone out of the bounds of the promised land and moved to Egypt for food during a famine. While there he had compromised Sarah his wife and put her in great danger, all to save his own skin. The subsequent trouble and embarrassment would, we might think, ensure that he would not want to repeat the event. Yet he did so.

What was wrong with Abraham? The following suggestions are only guesses, yet they are based on situations in which others of God's people made mistakes, so they can help us apply the lessons of the text to ourselves.

First, mountain-top experiences can make normal activity seem very flat and can therefore cause a spirit of restlessness. We know that after we have had an enjoyable spiritual event the regular activities of Christian living can seem very inferior. Instead of ascending the mountain we are trudging across the plain. In fact, we may get bored and decide to try something new, without any intention of going off the rails. Then, before we know where we are, we find ourselves in a situation where we have to compromise our gospel witness.

Second, while Abraham had gone through a mountain-top experience, he had also known serious spiritual disappointment. Mamre did not hold only good memories for him. In addition, it had been the place where he had interceded with God and not received all that he had asked. Only Lot had been delivered from divine judgement in response to Abraham's prayers. The disappointment may have been not that his prayer request had failed, but that he had not adequately assessed the spiritual state of Lot's family. He had assumed that Lot's family were of the same mind as their father, but they were not. A discovery of spiritual ignorance or an inaccurate perception will lead in one of two directions: either we ask God to teach us his will, or we begin walking in the wrong path.

Third, Abraham did not remind himself that the roots of past sins were still in his heart. It is generally the case that sins show themselves in particular circumstances. For example, a tendency to lose one's temper will usually be demonstrated in a situation of provocation; it is not likely to happen if such provocation is absent. A man with that tendency may go for years without being provoked greatly and he, as well as others, may think he has overcome it. Then, all of a sudden, he loses his temper and everybody knows about it. The reality of the situation is that he has not been putting spiritual weedkiller on the noxious plant in his soul:

praying about it specifically, starving it of what would strengthen it, and endeavouring to replace it with the grace that is the opposite of a bad temper. After the previous outburst, perhaps he attacked the weed with vigour, but slowly with the passing of time he has become less diligent, and eventually the weed has regrown and is ready to show itself.

It is true to say that the roots of every sin are in each person's heart. That is why Paul tells his readers not to steal and Peter demands that his readers do not commit murder. Given the right circumstances, none of us know what we are capable of doing. We must therefore spray spiritual weedkiller over our whole heart in order to prevent an unexpected fall. Yet we also know that each of us is prone to particular sins and therefore we must each concentrate on dealing continually with such sins. In Abraham's case, he seems to have possessed a sinful timidity at times (we should bear in mind that our weak points can often be very close to our strong points, and while Abraham was often brave in faith, he could show its opposite at times). We should not be surprised if those who have done great things for God show timidity when they cease to trust in God. Their strength was in the Lord, and what strength can such people have if they no longer have the Lord's strength? Abraham's timidity led to other sins such as self-centredness, lying to Abimelech, and a willingness to put Sarah in danger.

The faithfulness of God to Abimelech

The narrator describes a vision Abimelech received from God (v. 3). In the vision, the Lord informed Abimelech that he was in danger of fatal divine judgement because of his imminent adultery (he and his tribe had already received temporal judgements in the sense that God had prevented pregnancies, although it is doubtful if Abimelech had connected the lack of children with the presence of Sarah in his harem). Abimelech responded by saying that he had acted in ignorance and had been deceived by Abraham (vv. 4–5). The Lord informed the Philistine ruler that divine favour had kept him from committing sin (v. 6). Later details in the chapter reveal that Abimelech was a godly ruler, which in a sense is not surprising because there was an awareness of the true God in that geographical area, as can be seen with Melchizedek. There are several lessons to take note of in this dialogue between God and Abimelech.

First, we can see that sometimes ignorance is not accepted as a valid excuse. We may respond by saying that this is very unfair. Yet we should observe that Abimelech's ignorance was based on an assumption that Abraham was telling the truth. Imagine a man who borrows some money from the bank in order to enter into a financial partnership with another person. Later he finds out that his partner has swindled him out of the money he received from the bank. If he goes to the bank manager and suggests forgetting about repaying the loan because he did not know that his partner was corrupt, the bank manager will respond by saying that he should have checked out his partner's character and that it was wrong to have remained ignorant in such an important situation. Likewise, it was possible for Abimelech to have found out the truth regarding Abraham and Sarah. If we find ourselves in a wrong situation in which it was possible for us to have found out the truth about it, God will not accept our plea of ignorance. For example, there are many details in the Bible that we do not know but should know, and our ignorance of these is culpable.

Second, despite the fact that Abimelech was responsible to an extent for his ignorance, the Lord still showed grace to him by preventing him from sinning against Sarah. In a secret way, the Lord had overruled all the king's intentions and preserved him from sin. Yet because he was responsible for the danger he was in, Abimelech had to correct the situation, as otherwise he would undergo divine judgement.

Third, Abimelech discovered that there is a path of grace out of the darkest situation. Correcting it would result in him being the recipient of blessings linked to intercession with God: 'Now then, return the man's wife, for he is a prophet, so that he will pray for you, and you shall live' (v. 7). This is an amazing feature of God's workings. There was a path of grace even in circumstances in which human wilfulness (in the case of Abraham) and human carelessness (in the case of Abimelech) had created problems. This is a great encouragement. Apparently there are places on earth where the darkness is so dense the sun cannot shine through. In the spiritual world, however, there is no situation so dark that the Sun of righteousness cannot penetrate it with his warm beams of grace.

Abimelech on the path of grace

Having received his instructions from the Lord, Abimelech resolved to follow them. What did he do? His first step was to inform his servants of the situation (v. 8). In other words, he confessed to them that his carelessness had placed them all in a position of possible divine judgement. Their response was very appropriate: they were afraid of God's anger—the response we should expect in a community where there was a fear of God. There is an important lesson for us here as far as this community identity is concerned: the action of Abimelech had affected the whole community. Similarly, sin unrepented of by one person can affect a whole church. I cannot say that any of my sins have not affected anyone else. Others are not guilty of my sins, certainly, but sadly my sins may deprive a congregation of some blessings. This is a very important motive for personal as well as communal repentance.

Second, Abimelech confronted Abraham over his sin: 'What have you done to us? And how have I sinned against you, that you have brought on me and my kingdom a great sin? You have done to me things that ought not to be done' (v. 9). In addition, the king asked a very pertinent question of embarrassed Abraham: 'What did you see, that you did this thing?' (v. 10). It is as if he said, 'Abraham, I have tried to organize my kingdom in a way that is pleasing to God. What did you see that indicated otherwise?' The path of grace requires honest dealings by those who are on it. Abimelech's method should be noted: instead of pronouncing a negative judgement on Abraham's wrong ways, he asked questions designed to enable Abraham to explain why he had behaved in such a way.

Third, Abimelech showed great generosity towards Abraham: he 'took sheep and oxen, and male servants and female servants, and gave them to Abraham, and returned Sarah his wife to him. And Abimelech said, "Behold, my land is before you; dwell where it pleases you"' (vv. 14–15). The king's response is a practical example of the divine principle that, where sin abounded, grace did much more abound. A willingness to give to and share with those who have caused us pain and trouble is a marvellous sign of grace. Of course, it is very God-like to do so; after all, he gives to and shares with those who have rebelled against his rule and despised his grace.

Fourth, Abimelech showed he was a man of compassionate sensitivity when he went out of his way to ensure that everyone was aware that Sarah had not committed any sin in this prolonged situation: 'To Sarah he said, "Behold, I have given your brother a thousand pieces of silver. It is a sign of your innocence in the eyes of all who are with you, and before everyone you are vindicated"' (v. 16). While this action may only have been an expression of civility, it also indicates that the king had learned the important lesson of being careful in all his actions, and therefore he ensured that Sarah's good name was protected. It is a very encouraging sign when a person shows that he or she has profited from divine warnings.

Abraham on the path of grace

Abraham's response contains two aspects of repentance: one regarding recent sin and the other regarding distant sin. The recent sin was a wrong assessment he had made of the community, an assessment that was based on fear. He had wrongly assumed that no one in Gerar at that time feared God and that therefore he would be killed by them (v. 11). The distant confession concerned a decision he had made before he left Ur decades previously, when he asked his wife to pretend to be his sister when necessary (vv. 12–13). Some commentators regard Abraham's explanation as rather lame, but I don't see why his words cannot be taken as expressing repentance for two wrong outlooks that he had. If his words were not true expressions of repentance, it would be very surprising that the Lord then listened to his subsequent prayer.

Having repented, Abraham resumed his role as a prophet of God. His voice had been silent all the time he had been living in deception. But the moment he repented, his lips were opened and, even more amazing, his intercession on behalf of Abimelech and his household was heard. Abraham experienced the truth of Psalm 51:12–15 long before the words were penned by David:

Restore to me the joy of your salvation,
  and uphold me with a willing spirit.
Then I will teach transgressors your ways,
  and sinners will return to you.
Deliver me from bloodguiltiness, O God,
  O God of my salvation,
  and my tongue will sing aloud of your righteousness.
O Lord, open my lips,
  and my mouth will declare your praise.

The incident closes with the beautiful spectacle of the Philistine king of Gerar and the father of the faithful acting appropriately in the presence of God. The obvious lesson from this passage is that repentance restores us in God's sight, and when it takes place it shows itself on the path of grace on which hostilities are removed, previous mistakes are forgiven, expressions of kindness are displayed, divinely given roles are acknowledged, and the future is once again bright. Abraham and

Abimelech's friendship would continue to develop, as later chapters in Genesis will show.

Before we end our consideration of this incident, observe the time when all this took place. In verse 8, Moses stresses that Abimelech rose early in the morning and revealed the problem to his people. When is the best time to repent? As soon as possible.

The God who keeps his promises (Gen. 21)

How does God fulfil his promises? There are many answers to that question, and the author of Genesis details three divine methods in Genesis 21. First, the Lord sometimes fulfils his promises by a miraculous action, as he did in the case of the birth of Isaac. Second, God often keeps a promise in answer to a specific prayer, as he did in taking care of Hagar and Ishmael. Third, he regularly fulfils his promises by working in providence to increase the spread of his kingdom, and we can see this in the request of Abimelech to make a covenant with Abraham.

Keeping a promise through a miracle

Readers of Genesis have by now read about many events that occurred between the first promise given to Abraham concerning the birth of a son and the divine fulfilment of that promise. Of course, they do not have to wait as long as Abraham and Sarah did—thirty years. Yet eventually God did keep this particular promise and he gave them a son. The clear lesson from the prolonged period of three decades is that God's people usually have to exercise patience. There are several reasons why God sometimes works in this way. One is to remind us that he is sovereign, while another is to teach us that he knows the best time to work. A further reason is that the delay makes it very clear that the action is divine and could not have been brought about by our own resources.

So how should we respond when we are the beneficiaries of a divine blessing? The response of Abraham and Sarah to the birth of Isaac shows us what we should do. First, the reception of this blessing stimulated their obedience, as seen in two ways: the name that Abraham gave to his son and the act of circumcision that he performed on his son. God had previously instructed Abraham that he should call his son Isaac (17:19), which means 'laughter'. No doubt Abraham rejoiced when he gave this name to his son (21:3). God had also instructed him regarding the necessity of his male descendants being circumcised (17:12). The obedience of Abraham to this command (21:4) tells us that the reception of a divine miracle does not allow us to ignore or disobey God's commandments.

A church gathering is full of miracles—individuals who have undergone a greater miraculous birth than the birth of Isaac. Regeneration, or the giving of spiritual life, is superior to the experience of childbirth that Sarah went through. Our response to the wonderful miracle of regeneration should be similar to the two features displayed by the parents of Isaac: grateful rejoicing and eager obedience to God's commandments.

Second, the reception of a divine blessing increased their sense of wonder. Their amazement is clearly expressed in the words of Sarah in verses 6 and 7: 'God has made laughter for me; everyone who hears will laugh over me … Who would have said to Abraham that Sarah would nurse children? Yet I have borne him a son in his old age.'

Keeping a promise by answering prayer

About three years after the birth of Isaac, the day came when he was weaned, and it was a notable social occasion (v. 8). Abraham would have planned the event carefully, but he had no idea what was going to happen. Ishmael, by now a teenager (he was fourteen years older than Isaac), was caught by Sarah mocking Isaac, and it was so bad that she insisted Abraham remove Hagar and Ishmael from their community (vv. 9–10). Paul tells us that Ishmael's attitude was a form of persecution of Isaac (Gal. 4:29). Ishmael's words and taunts were almost certainly connected to this public display of Isaac as the heir, and Sarah resented his sinful comments. No doubt part of her reaction was caused by motherly affection; yet there was probably more to why she said what she did. Calvin was of the opinion that 'her tongue and mind were governed by a secret impulse of the Spirit, and that this whole affair was directed by the providence of God'.[1]

Sarah's demand seems very cruel to us, but it was accepted practice at that time to ensure that rivals to an heir were moved away. Abraham himself did this later regarding the sons he had by Keturah (25:1–6), so Sarah's request was not unusual and would not have caused any public disrepute to Abraham.

A PRAYER OF ABRAHAM

Abraham initially did not sense that the Lord would use this incident to ensure his purpose regarding Isaac would come to pass. To begin with, Abraham was very displeased with Sarah's ultimatum (v. 11). Yet I suspect that he prayed to God about the matter, which explains why God spoke to him about it and confirmed that her words were correct (vv. 12–13). This is the best way to respond to surprises. We should not trust our initial reaction, even if it seems appropriate. Instead we should always seek God's counsel on the issue. Calvin's insightful comment regarding Sarah's words is a reminder to us to be very careful how we respond to statements which, at first, may seem out of place.

In any case, Abraham received divine guidance about what to do and he obeyed God's requirement as soon as possible: 'So Abraham rose early in the morning and took bread and a skin of water and gave it to Hagar, putting it on her shoulder, along with the child, and sent her away. And she departed and wandered in the wilderness of Beersheba' (v. 14). It has been observed that the provision he gave her was very little, and some have suggested that by this means Abraham wanted to keep her close by so that he could provide her with further supplies in the future. If that was the case, it would suggest that natural ties hindered him from fully believing what God had promised: that God would take care of Ishmael and make him into a great nation (v. 13). Alternatively, Abraham may have wanted them nearby in order to keep an eye on them, perhaps to prevent them from being attacked by tribes or affected by sinful practices found in that area (as had happened with Lot).

A PRAYER OF ISHMAEL

We have in this story a mention of prayer that may seem a bit surprising. Perhaps we might expect to be told that Abraham prayed for Hagar and Ishmael, or that Hagar prayed for her son in his physical distress through lack of water. Instead the text says that Ishmael prayed: 'God heard the voice of the boy' (v. 17). We don't know what Ishmael was saying in his prayer, although he would have observed his father praying and would therefore have known how to address God. Whatever Ishmael said, he was heard by God. Sometimes it takes a crisis to bring a person to his or her senses, and perhaps Ishmael realized that his wrong behaviour had caused their expulsion from the household of his father. The incident is a marvellous example of the grace of God because here the one who had mocked the heir received kindness from the God who had given that position to the heir. Although he could not have Isaac's place, Ishmael would receive his own place from God several years later, in response to the prayer he made here. So God kept a promise by listening to the prayers of a sinful individual in need.

Ishmael was denied the place God had sovereignly chosen to give to Isaac. Yet this did not mean he was abandoned by God. Moses informs us that God was with Ishmael as he grew up (v. 20). It is possible to interpret that summary statement as meaning that God took care of Ishmael without providing him with saving grace. However, Matthew Henry's comment regarding Ishmael's rejection is wise: 'We are not sure that it was his eternal ruin. It is presumption to say that all those who are left out of the external dispensation of God's covenant are therefore excluded from all his mercies: those may be saved who are not thus honoured. However, we are sure it was not his temporal ruin.'[2] What we do know is that Ishmael prayed in his distress, was heard by God on that occasion, and that God was with him to ensure that he received what was promised to him by God. Ishmael's experience illustrated the meaning of his name: 'God hears.'

A PRAYER OF HAGAR

I assume that Hagar was praying as well. It would be very surprising if she did not, given the circumstances she was in. Perhaps she did not use words: perhaps only groans came from her devastated spirit. What is clear is that her state of soul caused Heaven to respond to her circumstances.

This was the second time Hagar found herself in this kind of situation. On the previous occasion, when she had fled from Sarah, she had received divine instructions to return to Abraham's household. Now, because of divine instructions given to Abraham, she had been put out of his camp. I suspect she was confused, and her confusion could have led her to forget that there was a God whose eyes were on her.

In addition to her possible confusion arising from God's different instructions, her circumstances had become very difficult. Her son, about whom God had given her great promises on that previous occasion (16:10–12), was about to die (vv. 15–16). It looked as if God's pledge to her would not be fulfilled; in fact, it looked as if God was against her. What could she say to him? All she could do was weep. But although she found the heavens as brass, there was One who collected her tears in his bottle and who had not forgotten her (Ps. 56:8).

On this occasion Hagar received heavenly guidance about Ishmael (just as Abraham had done about him). The passage states that the person who spoke to her from heaven was 'the angel of God' (v. 17). On the previous occasion, when she had also received heavenly guidance, the One who spoke to her was 'the angel of the LORD', which we suggested was a common Old Testament designation of the Son of God. In this instance, the name of the heavenly being retains the definite article, which indicates that he is special, and he also says that he will make Ishmael into a great nation, which is beyond the ability of a created angel. So it is the same divine Person who is addressing Hagar for the second time and who comes to her aid.

The Son of God spoke compassionately and tenderly to her before repeating his previous promise about her son (v. 18). Here is a wonderful reminder that the Lord Jesus cares for those to whom he has given promises. He is aware of their fears and comes to comfort and console them. Having repeated to her his promise about the future, he also provided for her needs in the present by showing her that a well was close at hand (v. 19). He knew all along that the well was there, and in his providence he had taken distressed Hagar to a location where he could meet her need, a reminder to her that he could provide for them in the future. This is an important perspective to retain: in our troubles the Lord leads the blind by a way they know not and often brings them, in their distress and concern, to the very place which they think is the worst but is actually where he will give great blessings.

I suspect Hagar did not again need another special word from heaven. She could live out her days aware that One in heaven was taking care of her, that despite their unusual providences God was with her son as they adjusted to life away from Abraham. In due course she found him a wife, probably from among her relations in Egypt. But in her experience, she had discovered that God used prayer—that of her son and herself—to fulfil his promises. This incident of a thirsty teenager and a distressed mother therefore teaches us that God answers prayer and thereby keeps his promises.

Keeping a promise through growing his kingdom

Years previously, God had made a promise to Abraham that his seed would be a blessing to the nations. Readers of Genesis have been waiting to see this promise fulfilled, and now Moses points out that shortly after the birth of Isaac a powerful Philistine group voluntarily aligned themselves with Abraham because they had observed that God was with him (vv. 22–23). Their desire for identification with Abraham is all the more surprising because, as we observed in a previous chapter, Abraham had been deceptive in his previous contact with this group of Philistines. Yet on that occasion he had discovered that they feared God.

Since Abraham was at the centre of God's plan of salvation, readers of Genesis would assume that others with an interest in God's mercy would desire to join his servant in a public manner. It is evident that Abimelech realized that Abraham was going to be present in the land for a long time, which is why he asked that future generations of his people might receive blessings through Abraham. Abimelech and Phicol were willing to confess that the land belonged to a man who at that time seemed to have very little in comparison to what they had. But they did not judge things by the sight of their eyes; instead they looked ahead with the eyes of faith and recognized that God would certainly bless Abraham. This is how we are to respond to the gospel. On a human level, the church of Christ seems insignificant. Yet the fact is that the future belongs to it and not to those who seem currently to have a place of prominence. Heavenly wisdom states that we should by faith identify ourselves with the despised people of God.

We may wonder why Abraham made such a fuss about a well in Beersheba when he brought up the matter with Abimelech (v. 25). It is likely that Abraham had dug this well (although some scholars think it is the well Hagar used). Abraham pointed out that his ownership of the well should not be disputed with those who wanted to identify themselves as his friends. They had to confess that the land belonged to him, not them.

Abraham's response to the treaty with Abimelech was worship. He planted a grove as a place where he could engage in worship and call upon the name of God (v. 33). Candlish suggests that the grove was designed for use by both Abraham and Abimelech: 'And there, from time to time, the two friends might meet, as members of the same communion, having now a common faith, a common hope, a common love, to call in common "on the name of the Lord, the everlasting God".'[3] Genesis 21 reveals that Abraham had many reasons for giving thanks. His God had kept his promises concerning Isaac, had provided for Hagar and Ishmael, and had created permanent peace between Abraham and Abimelech. And what God did for the father of the faithful, he does for those who follow in his steps.

NOTES

1   Calvin, *Genesis*, p. 543.
2   Henry, *Commentary*, on Gen. 21:13–14.
3   Candlish, *Studies in Genesis*, p. 344.

Offering up Isaac (Gen. 22)

S ome time has passed, perhaps a few years, since the previous recorded incident in Genesis 21. It is difficult to work out exactly how old Isaac was by this time. He is called a 'boy' in verse 5, but that term could indicate a teenager. In any case, he was old enough to be able to walk for three days from Beersheba in the south to Moriah, which is probably the area around Jerusalem and about fifty or so miles away, and to understand the elements and significance of a sacrifice to God.

There is a link between God's command to Abraham concerning erecting an altar and Abraham's previous activity of building altars throughout the land. When the patriarch erected those altars he was claiming for himself and his seed the land promised to them by God. Now the God who gave these promises came and told Abraham to perform an activity which would reveal whether or not he was prepared to show that the Lord had total authority over him.

Abraham tested to the limit

The first thought that arises from this incident is that sometimes God asks his people to make great and costly sacrifices. We are familiar with stories of missionaries and others who have left the comfort of their home surroundings to serve God in harsh and inhospitable terrains, often without receiving much evidence of success. Others have been called to a life of pain in which they have endured prolonged periods of distress, without being able to see the point of it all. Such sacrifices are long-term, and perhaps those making them eventually get used to them and discover some spiritual benefits from them, such as intercessory prayer and patient submission to the will of God. On the other hand, some people experience sudden tragedy or catastrophe, with no explanation other than the reality that they are liable to all the miseries of this life. Christians lose their employment and Christian businessmen see their companies go bankrupt. Other Christians are hurt in sudden outbreaks of war or in earthquakes.

Yet there is a difference between these cases and what was demanded of Abraham here. Why so? Because Abraham was asked not only to perform the difficult task of killing his son, but also to destroy what seemed to be the future of God's kingdom. The patriarch had been told many times by God that the line of the future Messiah was through Isaac. Now he was told to carry out an action that would result in that line being aborted almost at its beginning. Such a command would have seemed worse than unrealistic to most thinking people. Yet Abraham determined to proceed along the path of obedience.

Before we make some comments on Abraham's response, it is worth noting that God's action here is actually a comforting one because it indicates that he is concerned about the spiritual state of each of his people. We are not to imagine that he tests us only occasionally; he tests us often in order to reveal how we are growing in grace. Sometimes he tests us by allowing the devil to tempt us. At other times, God tests us with prosperity; on occasions, as with Job, he tests us by adversity. The point to note is that divine testing is a sign of his commitment to his people, a reminder that he is watching over us, concerned about our spiritual development and holiness.

It is also worth noting that what God expects of his people is worship. Abraham was commanded to perform this unusual task as an expression of worship. God told him to offer Isaac as a burnt offering, which is a picture of total dedication in that all of the sacrifice was consumed on the altar. It may be that Abraham had become too fond of Isaac, as some authors suggest, and his dedication to God was not so apparent. I'm not sure about that. But it is the case that each action of a disciple of Christ should be an act of worship in which our devotion to him is clearly seen.

Abraham responds in faith

Abraham responded to this divine charge in faith. This explains the unusual lack of disagreement with such a request, or even a downright refusal to obey it. Since it was a response of faith, the example of Abraham is a reminder that sometimes faith in God has to battle with natural affection. On what was Abraham's faith based? It was based on his knowledge of God; and we can see four features of that knowledge in Abraham's response.

The first reason why he proceeded was because he trusted God. It would have been easy for Abraham to conclude that God was contradicting himself by giving a commandment that went against his previous promises. Instead he assessed the situation by what he understood of God and not by what he did not understand about God. He knew, for example, that his God could perform miracles because he had performed a great one in the birth of Isaac. Therefore Abraham deduced that if another miracle was called for, God would perform it. The author of Hebrews tells us that Abraham did believe that God would perform a miracle: he was sure that God would raise Isaac from the dead (Heb. 11:19). Faith always says that God's wisdom has the answer.

A second reason why Abraham proceeded was because he recognized that God can do what he wants with what belongs to him. Of course, such a statement is easy to say when all is going well, but it takes great faith to say it when troubles are abounding. Yet this is how Job also reacted when he lost everything: 'Naked I came from my mother's womb, and naked shall I return. The LORD gave, and the LORD has taken away; blessed be the name of the LORD' (Job 1:21). Abraham had the same attitude and was prepared to proceed on the basis of it. Faith always says that God is sovereign.

A third reason why Abraham proceeded was because he recognized that somehow in the darkness God was still good. As Robert Candlish noted,

But, in the eye of faith, the venerable patriarch was still, even in this hour of terror, looking up to God, and reposing with unshaken confidence on that goodness which, during a long and harassed life, had never deceived or forsaken him. The same humble and holy trust in God, as his benefactor and his friend, which had thus far led him in safety, still triumphed over every doubt. Harsh as the decree might appear, he knew by much experience that God had never yet commanded him to his hurt.[1]

A fourth way in which Abraham's faith responded during this time of severe testing was to consider the faithfulness of God. As the patriarch considered the way in which God had led him, he could easily see how faithful God had been, as Candlish notes:

he felt that the faithfulness of God must be as secure in the time to come as he had ever found it in time past. The cloud, indeed, might be dark which veiled the divine proceedings from his view; but it was not so dark as to cast a single shadow over his heart. He still trusted in the Lord as implicitly as when first he abandoned his father's house, casting himself on the Lord's protection.[2]

I suggest that these four responses of faith—trust in God's wisdom, belief in God's sovereign right to do what he wishes with his own, confidence in God's permanent goodness and affirmation of God's certain faithfulness—enabled Abraham to proceed with this severe test.

Blessings of the testing

It was a very hard and unusual testing for Abraham. We know the story and are aware that God had an alternative plan all the time, but Abraham did not know this until he reached the climactic moment and God called from heaven instructing him not to slay his son. There are several other lessons we can deduce from this incident.

Some may wonder why such an advanced and experienced believer should be asked by God to perform such a strange act of obedience. Spurgeon provides an explanation:

Abraham was a man whose life gave good evidence of his faith in Jehovah; but the Lord is a jealous God, and he loves to have still more evidence of the fidelity of his people. He hungers after clear proofs from them that they really are his; and he works in them by his grace until he casts out all other loves, and all other confidences, that he may have the whole of their hearts, and that they may love him and trust him supremely.[3]

We can see this divine interest in the words of the angel of the Lord when he said later to Abraham: 'Do not lay your hand on the boy or do anything to him, for now I know that you fear God, seeing you have not withheld your son, your only son, from me' (v. 12). A right response to divine testing brought not only assurance to Abraham, but also pleasure to God. When believers know that God's smile is upon them, their sense of joy increases.

Next, we should observe that the angel of the Lord (who was a divine being himself, the Son of God before he became a man) reminded Abraham of great divine promises. He said in verses 15–18:

By myself I have sworn, declares the LORD, because you have done this and have not withheld your son, your only son, I will surely bless you, and I will surely multiply your offspring as the stars of heaven and as the sand that is on the seashore. And your offspring shall possess the gate of his enemies, and in your offspring shall all the nations of the earth be blessed, because you have obeyed my voice.

Much of what is said here had been said before to Abraham, especially about the number of his descendants and the universal blessing that would come. A new detail was that his seed would triumph over all enemies. What happened to Abraham is a sample of what happens to tried believers after the test has been completed. Jesus draws near and soothes away the pain of the trial by applying his sweet promises with greater clarity and detail. The Saviour who seemed so far away draws near and comforts his servants during a time of precious fellowship.

Further, the test gave Abraham an insight into the future Father–Son transaction that would take place centuries later at Calvary. I like the suggestion made by several commentators that the background to this event was a prayer made by Abraham for information about how his seed would be a source of blessing to the world. If this conjecture is true, and it would be very unlikely for Abraham not to have thought about it, the Lord gave him a personal lesson on the significance of Calvary.

Certainly Jesus stated in John 8:56 that Abraham rejoiced to see the day of Christ. The Saviour's words do not say that Abraham merely looked forward to that day, although that would be true; Jesus says that Abraham 'saw' it, and there is no other incident recorded from the life of Abraham that gave him such a profound insight as this one, when he was asked to offer his son as a sacrifice.

When we turn our eyes to the cross we see the Father and the Son making their way there together. Their journey did not begin at Beersheba and it did not end at a physical location like Moriah. Instead it began in heaven; the Father was with his Son as he journeyed from there to earth and he remained with him throughout the years of his earthly journey. Even when all others had forsaken him, Jesus said that the Father was still with him (John 16:32). But the Father and the Son reached a dreadful point in their journey when the Father spared not his own Son but delivered him up for us all (Rom. 8:32). This did not happen only visibly in this world, the place where the Father brought his Son to the 'dust of death' (Ps. 22:15). Externally it happened at Calvary, but the place of fatherly abandonment took place within the Saviour's own experience.

Abraham saw that the Father would bruise his Son in order that blessings might come to the nations of the world. And just as he had believed that God would raise Isaac from the dead, so he saw that the Father would raise his own Son from the dead. In a sense, at Moriah, Abraham saw the purposes of God the Father as far as giving his Son was concerned; he saw the pain of the Father as he gave his Son; and he saw the pleasure of the Father in providing his Son as the substitute for sinners.

Finally, the testing gave Abraham a message to pass on to others. This message is seen in the name he gave to the location: Jehovah Jireh, which means 'the Lord will provide', no doubt linked to his own words in verse 8: 'God will provide for himself the lamb for a burnt offering, my son.' Abraham could tell others that his God never brings a test without providing a means of release. In addition, he could tell them that the Lord would yet provide his own Son to be the Saviour of sinners, the One who would bring universal blessing to untold numbers of generations in the future. Many did listen to Abraham; we are told in verse 14 that others were repeating his words centuries later: 'as it is said to this day, "On the mount of the LORD it shall be provided."' Let's listen to him.

NOTES

1   Candlish, *Studies in Genesis*, p. 368.
2   Ibid., pp. 368–369.
3   C. H. Spurgeon, *Spurgeon's Sermons*, Volume 31, 'Abraham's Trial: A Lesson for Believers', sermon on Gen. 22:1.

The death of a princess (Gen. 23)

As we can see from Genesis 23:1, Sarah lived for thirty-seven years after the birth of Isaac. Although she had been an old woman when she experienced the fulfilment of God's promise, she had the enjoyment of it for a longer period than she had had to wait for it to happen. She was ten years younger than Abraham, so she was sixty-five when she came with him to Canaan. There she had to wait twenty-five years for Isaac to be born, which happened when she was ninety, but for the rest of her life she enjoyed the living evidence that her God was an almighty and faithful God.

So Sarah had her days of spiritual enjoyment. She and her husband had been the originators of the organized community of God's people. Many believers had lived before her time, and we read about some of them in the early chapters of Genesis; however, they were not organized together, as Abraham's descendants came to be. I think this may explain an omission in the account of the death of Sarah. Several times in Genesis the description of a believer's death includes the beautiful clause 'and he was gathered to his people'. It is used of Abraham (25:8), Ishmael (25:17), Isaac (35:29) and Jacob (49:29, 33); and in later books it is also used of Moses (Deut. 32:50) and Aaron (Num. 20:24, 26). It is not, however, used of Sarah. A possible reason for the omission is her gender, since the clause is not used elsewhere of a woman. Yet it may also be the case that Sarah had no people with whom to be gathered because she was the first of the chosen people to die. Perhaps the author of Genesis is making this point and is highlighting her role as a founding member of the community.

Yet despite her prominence in God's kingdom and the great privileges she had received from God, she had to face the last enemy, and when that day came it was not her prominence or her privileges that helped her. The only reason for her entrance into heaven was the fact that she believed in the promised Deliverer, who was to be one of her descendants. She had looked ahead to his coming and died strong in faith, as the writer of Hebrews tells us:

These all [including Sarah] died in faith, not having received the things promised, but having seen them and greeted them from afar, and having acknowledged that they were strangers and exiles on the earth. For people who speak thus make it clear that they are seeking a homeland. If they had been thinking of that land from which they had gone out, they would have had opportunity to return. But as it is, they desire a better country, that is, a heavenly one. Therefore God is not ashamed to be called their God, for he has prepared for them a city (Heb. 11:13–16).

The Bible does not say whether Sarah's death was comfortable or painful, whether she died suddenly or after a long illness. Such details would be of interest if we had them, but in a sense they are only circumstantial. What mattered was not whether she died bravely or whether she died solitarily, by herself. From the Bible's perspective, all that matters is that she died in faith. If her earthly husband was absent because of legitimate reasons, her eternal Husband, the Saviour who is the Son of God, was present with her. No doubt her earthly husband had carried her through many a flood and other dangers, but he could not take her over the gulf of death. But she had long known the One who would, and when she came to the edge of the river of death, he was there to take her safely across.

Expressing his faith in God

Throughout the account of his life in Genesis, we see that Abraham came through many situations in which he had to express his faith in God.

Sometimes this was accompanied by repentance, as when God protected him from the consequences of his natural cowardliness when he was willing to compromise the chastity of his wife (12:10–20; 20:1–18). At other times, he fought against powerful foes and rescued his nephew Lot (ch. 14) or prayed earnestly for God to show mercy and not destroy Sodom and Gomorrah (18:22–33). In each situation, though, Abraham was at some stage brought to show that he was a man of faith. And this is the point of the incident here with the purchase of a cave: the cave was an expression of faith in the promises of God.

It was clearly a sad day in Abraham's experience when his beloved wife passed away. She had shared with him almost every stage in his pilgrimage. Perhaps, as he wept over her, his mind went back to their life in Ur of the Chaldees and to the day when he informed her that he had received a visit from the Lord of glory (Acts 7:2). His thoughts would wander over the years since then, sad that they would never again in this world speak together about the things of God.

There is a biblical way of expressing grief. Paul told the Thessalonians that, while they were not to sorrow as those who had no hope, they were still to sorrow for the separation (1 Thes. 4:13). Abraham expressed his sorrow personally, privately and purposely. Personally, he made his way to her tent; privately, he grieved there for her; and as he did so he purposely determined to show others that his sorrow was grounded in faith in God. The way Abraham chose to express his sorrow was by buying a private burial place. The story of how this came about also reveals other aspects of the faith of Abraham.

Evidence of his faith

The first sign of Abraham's faith expressed during this incident is his self-description in verse 4, when he spoke to his neighbours who had probably come to sympathize with him over his loss. He reminded them that he was 'a sojourner and foreigner' among them, and this description is picked up in Hebrews 11:13 as a statement of faith. In the context of an experience which is common to all people—the death of a beloved spouse—Abraham humbly stated that he was different from his kind, courteous neighbours. By calling himself a 'sojourner' Abraham revealed that he had not yet found his permanent home, and by calling himself a 'foreigner' he said that he was not yet among his own people. Of course, he was using everyday terminology in a spiritual manner: he was not insulting his neighbours, and it is clear from their response that they were not offended. Abraham was indicating that he looked at life from a heavenly perspective and saw himself through that lens. He was looking for another country, a perfect one; and for another people, a holy one.

A second feature of Abraham's faith was his willingness to put up with the situations he faced, and his humility in them. God had given the whole of Canaan to Abraham and his descendants, yet here he was without an inch of ground. He didn't even have a suitable spot to use as a family burial area and therefore had to ask his neighbours for help. It would have been easy for Abraham to chafe and wonder why God's promises regarding the land had not been fulfilled. Instead he chose to act according to the current providence of God and to not let circumstances undermine his hold of the promises. A similar dilemma faces many Christians today. They know that they are the heirs of all things with Jesus, yet many of them don't know where their next meal will come from. But faith does not allow the difficulties of the present to nullify the realities of the promised future.

A third feature of Abraham's faith is revealed in the Hittites' response to him. Their assessment of him was that he was 'a prince of God' (sometimes translated as 'mighty prince'). During the years Abraham had lived among them they had had the opportunity of weighing his life, and it was their unanimous conclusion that he was one of God's favourites. This does not mean that they were fellow-worshippers with him of the true God. Rather it points to the fact that even pagans can recognize a person on whom God's favour rests. Given the unusual birth of Isaac it would have been hard for them to have concluded otherwise, yet they bore a striking testimony to one who regarded himself as nothing but 'dust and ashes' (18:27). So highly did they esteem him that they gave him the choicest of their tombs.

Fourth, Abraham's faith is revealed in the manner he conducted the bargaining process for the purchase of the field and cave of Machpelah. He insisted on paying the full price and having the transaction witnessed. At first, his response seems surprising because Ephron offered the field and the cave for nothing. Some speculate that Ephron was not sincere in his offer, but I don't think the passage suggests that was the case. Thy reason why Abraham insisted on the process was because he was looking ahead to a period when neither he nor they would be alive, when others might try to retake the tomb from his family. It is remarkable that the tomb remained in Abraham's family for many years: Jacob, who had not even been born when Sarah died, would be buried there when he died at the age of 147. I wonder what the descendants of Ephron thought when they saw Jacob buried there with all the honour of the Egyptians (Gen. 50:9–13). Abraham ensured that the cave and the field belonged to his family, no matter what happened in the future. And that burial place, where lies the dust of Abraham and Sarah, Isaac and Rebekah, Jacob and Leah, is still watched over by the King of heaven.

The symbolism of Machpelah

The burial of Sarah is the first recorded interment of a person in the Bible. The first mention of a particular thing in the Bible is usually of importance and indicates that the author wanted his readers to reflect on its significance. So here are some realities to which Machpelah points.

First, it reminds us that death brings destruction. Death is not a pleasant subject, but it is a real one. Abraham had to bury Sarah out of sight because of the changes that death would bring. Machpelah reminds readers that such destruction will happen even to those who are the recipients of God's promises.

Second, Machpelah speaks of the fact that God sometimes seems to take a long time to fulfil his promises. Perhaps Abraham and Sarah had wondered if they would live to see the arrival of the promised Messiah. Her death, and his later on, is a reminder that it was otherwise; that in fact there would be a long delay before the Messiah came. Machpelah speaks of this reality because within its bounds were the remains of some who died longing for the coming of the Saviour.

Third, Machpelah speaks of the different destinies of those who die. Sarah was not buried in despair or with a sense of futility; instead she was laid to rest by a family who believed in the future resurrection. That lonely cave became a sign of hope, and subsequent family members were buried there because they believed there would be a resurrection and reunion in the future.

Fourth, Machpelah was, in an unusual way, an act of dedication by Abraham. This was true as far as his duty to Sarah was concerned, but it was also true at a far higher level because he was putting the remains of his wife into the care of God until the resurrection morning came. It was an expression of confidence in the Lord by Abraham the man of faith. Earlier he had shown dedication when he was willing to offer up his son Isaac in obedience to God. Now Abraham showed his dedication by putting Sarah's remains into God's hands.

A wife for Isaac (Gen. 24)

Who is the story in this chapter about, and who is the central character in it? The story is about Isaac and how he found a wife, but he is not really the central figure of the account. A case can be made for Eliezar (who is probably the steward mentioned here); or perhaps the author wants readers to notice features in the characters of each person in the narrative. I will take this last option in order to consider what we are told.

Abraham: preserving the testimony

Throughout his account of Abraham's life Moses has been stressing that Abraham was a man of God who responded to each situation by faith. As we have observed in previous chapters, sometimes the required response involved repentance for a failure, as when he asked his wife to pretend she was his sister; or it involved exercising faith in distressing circumstances, as when he grieved for Sarah in faith when she died. Several of his decisions involved his son Isaac, such as Isaac's supernatural birth or the unusual commandment of God to offer Isaac as a sacrifice on Mount Moriah. Regarding these decisions about Isaac Abraham had to express faith without knowing all the details; for example, he did not know how his aged wife could give birth or when God would raise Isaac from the dead. Yet on each occasion he was present and at least able to observe what took place. Now, however, he comes to express faith in God for a situation for which he suspects he may not be long on earth in order to give advice to Isaac. It is not only faith concerning the unknown;

it is also faith that is aware of his absence from the scene. But he has to move forward and make provisions for Isaac by faith.

Abraham's response of faith involved assessing the situation and arranging the solution. His assessment was twofold: Isaac could not leave the land of promise and he could not marry one of the Canaanite women. For Isaac to marry seemed almost impossible, yet we know that faith in God often faces such situations. Yet the God in whom Abraham believed had already provided him with a man who was to help in this dilemma: his faithful steward was the God-given remedy. The fact is, God never arranges a test without providing, perhaps later in time, a means of solving the situation. Once again Abraham discovered that God could be trusted to take care of events. If Abraham had taken the easier option of arranging a wife locally for Isaac, a disaster would have occurred. But those who determine to obey in faith will find an opening provided by God.

Abraham was not expecting to live for much longer, but it is interesting that he lived long enough for his grandchildren to be teenagers. His death occurred when he was 175, by which point Isaac was seventy-five. Genesis 25:26 says that Isaac was sixty when his sons were born, which means that they were fifteen when Abraham died. So we can say that Abraham lived long enough to see the vindication of his faith that his God would provide a wife and descendants for Isaac in order to continue the testimony to God that was given to Abraham and his descendants.

Eliezar: the heart of a servant

Who could Abraham trust to fulfil this errand that would contribute to the ongoing development of God's kingdom? Abraham knew the very man: his steward; he is probably the Eliezar of Damascus mentioned by Abraham in Genesis 15:2. As we think about this steward, we should observe him not just as a servant of a man, but as a servant of God. Right away we can see an essential feature of the heart of a servant:

trustworthiness. How long does it take to build up such trust? Usually many years. How long does it take to lose it? Often one action.

A biblical example is Mark, the nephew of Barnabas. On Paul's first missionary journey, Mark, who had accompanied Paul and Barnabas as their servant, decided to give up and return home. His action meant that Paul did not trust him as a helper for the second missionary journey, which led to a disagreement between Paul and Mark's relative, Barnabas. Eventually Mark proved himself and became a companion, not only of Barnabas, but later also of Paul and Peter, and he even wrote one of the Gospels.

The remedy for Abraham's dilemma was for Eliezar to make his way to Haran and find a wife for Isaac from among the relatives of Abraham. Having received his instructions, the steward set off (v. 10). We should note that he took with him gifts that would enhance his master in the eyes of those he met. As we have just noted, the first qualification for a servant heart is trustworthiness; here is a second qualification: the inner desire that our master's name will be honoured. The gifts that the steward gave had to be in line with the words he used. He could not say that Abraham was a wealthy man but then give only trinkets as presents. The obvious application for our serving of God is that Christians will share the blessings which God has given to them in providence. Christians who live like misers send out the message that their Master is a miser. On the other hand, Christians who live a generous life tell others that their Master is generous.

Eventually Eliezar reached the location where Abraham's relatives lived and he found himself at a well (v. 11). His immediate reaction was to engage in prayer (vv. 12–14). We can imagine the situation: he knows he will see several women there (they will come to the well as part of their daily activities), so how will he know which one to speak to? Merely looking at them will not give him insight into their characters. Moses informs us that the steward engaged in a simple, straightforward prayer, yet one which contained a request that was not likely to be answered unless God compelled one of the women to perform it. A camel can drink twenty-five gallons of water, and the jar which a woman usually carried would hold three gallons. The woman sent in response to this prayer would have to volunteer to draw 250 gallons of water, which means that she would have to make over eighty trips to the well—all to meet the needs of a total stranger. Of course, his prayer was made in secret, and this is a reminder that the servant of God engages in secret prayer while doing other things.

Why did Eliezar make this unusual request? We have already mentioned one possible reason: that only God could cause a stranger to agree to such a request. In addition, Eliezar's request also indicated that he wanted a woman in whose heart God had been working, a woman whom God had taught to be kind, hospitable and marked by self-sacrifice. In other words, the servant's request showed that he wanted a spiritually suitable woman as a wife for Isaac.

Yet the servant knew that more information was needed before he could reveal the reason for his visit. It was possible that more than one woman would give the response for which he had prayed. Before he had left Abraham, the patriarch had told him to choose only a woman who was a relative of Isaac's (vv. 3–4). Therefore the servant rewarded the girl for her labour by giving her some gifts and then asked her who she was (v. 23). When he learned that she was the granddaughter of Nahor, the servant bowed in worship to the Lord (vv. 26–27). He confessed with wonder the faithfulness of God to Abraham and the guidance he, as the steward, had received personally. The heart of a servant acknowledges the goodness of God as soon as it is appropriate to do so.

Rebekah ran home and told her family what had happened (v. 28). Her brother Laban came and insisted that the visitor share their provisions. His words are beautiful—'Come in, O blessed of the Lord. Why do you stand outside? For I have prepared the house and a place for the camels'

(v. 31)—although, knowing what Genesis says later of Laban, his heart may have had ulterior motives. Yet his words must have been encouraging to the steward because they revealed that the Lord's name was known in this family.

After he had taken care of the animals, the servant once again showed that he had not forgotten his mission. Before he would satisfy his hunger he insisted on saying why he had come (v. 33). He rehearsed what had taken place when he received his commission from Abraham and explained his behaviour at the spring when Rebekah arrived there (vv. 34–49). The terms of his task meant he had to find out if Rebekah was available, and Laban and Bethuel indicated that she was. Again the servant revealed his piety by worshipping the Lord (v. 52; he also showed his concern for Abraham's honour by giving suitable gifts to Rebekah and her family, v. 53).

Everything had gone so smoothly, and the reader may be wondering if anything will go wrong in this romantic story. Sure enough, a test suddenly appeared for the servant. It came through the form of a reasonable request: that Rebekah wait for a couple of weeks before leaving her home (v. 55). After all, the visit of the servant was very sudden and this would give time for suitable arrangements to be made. Often the tests that servants of God stumble over are reasonable requests, sometimes even coming from relatives. Thankfully, the servant had one simple rule by which to assess all such suggestions: he said, 'If it hinders obedience to my master, I cannot go along with it.' From the servant's point of view, everything turned out well. Rebekah stated that she was willing to go with the steward.

There is one more detail from Eliezar's experience to ponder. When the caravan returned to the home of Abraham, the servant told Isaac (who was also his master) all that he had done (v. 66). In other words, he rendered his account of his service. No doubt Isaac was delighted with the faithfulness of his servant. At a far higher level, all servants of God (all believers) will yet render an account to their Master for how they have served him in this world. It will be wonderful if our service for Jesus is like Eliezar's service for Abraham and Isaac.

Rebekah: the girl who made a choice

As we have observed, Rebekah had been moulded in some ways in the knowledge of God. Her response to the call to go with Eliezar has often been likened to the response sinners should make to the gospel, and we can think about two details in that connection.

First, her response was based on what she had heard about Isaac and on the samples she had seen of his wealth. Similarly, sinners who turn to Jesus do so on the basis of what they have been told or have read, and what they have seen of God's wealth. Sinners hear about the mission of Jesus to save them and also see in the lives of others the riches of Christ's grace. Although Rebekah had never seen Isaac, she had enough evidence on which to base her decision. And so it is with any who hear the gospel and see it lived out in the lives of Christ's disciples.

Second, her response was given immediately because the servant would not consider any delay. In the gospel also the call is for an immediate response. Jesus demands instant faith in himself, such as when he called Levi, who was sitting at his tax booth, and demanded that he leave it and follow him—which Levi did. Perhaps Rebekah could have asked for more information, because it was true that she was ignorant of many details about Isaac. More information would be given to her on the journey. Likewise, we cannot make ignorance of the details about Jesus a reason for not following him. In any other walk of life, it is wise to check things out very carefully. But with regard to the gospel, it is folly to delay because none know if they will have enough time to investigate further, and instead of being saved through faith, such may be lost.

The death of Abraham (Gen. 25:1–11)

Moses, in this passage, brings to a close his account of the life of Abraham. In doing so, he briefly mentions how Abraham gave Isaac the rights to the inheritance. He ensured that this would happen by sending away from his camp the five sons he had by his second wife, Keturah, whom he had probably married after the death of Sarah. Some scholars, including Calvin, suggest that Abraham had married Keturah when Sarah was alive, but this is very unlikely as Sarah would not have allowed it, given her trouble with Hagar.

At first glance, Abraham's actions regarding these sons might seem unfair, but in reality what he did was set them free from a life of service to Isaac; I therefore suspect that they had no objections to their treatment by their father. We are not told how long before the death of Abraham this separation occurred. Given that Sarah died thirty-eight years before Abraham passed away, there was plenty of time for the sons of Keturah to grow up. They were probably in their twenties or thirties when they left Abraham's camp.

Promises fulfilled

Another reason for Moses' mention of these descendants through Keturah is to provide readers with evidence of God's fulfilled promise. In Genesis 17:4–5 God had said to Abraham, 'Behold, my covenant is with you, and you shall be the father of a multitude of nations. No longer shall your name be called Abram, but your name shall be Abraham, for I have made you the father of a multitude of nations.' The founders of several nations, each descended from Abraham, are mentioned in Genesis 25:1–4.

In addition, Moses informs his readers about the immediate descendants of Ishmael (vv. 12–18). As God had previously promised Abraham (17:20), Ishmael had twelve sons, each of whom began a family group and spread out throughout the region. I suppose Moses can be read as saying that Ishmael's descendants could be found everywhere, a visible reminder that God had kept his promise regarding this son of Abraham, even as far as the number of his children was concerned. It is worth noting that, centuries later, Isaiah predicted that spiritual blessings would be given to the descendants of Ishmael during the days of the Messiah: 'All the flocks of Kedar shall be gathered to you; the rams of Nebaioth shall minister to you; they shall come up with acceptance on my altar, and I will beautify my beautiful house' (Isa. 60:7).

A good question to ponder at the funeral of a believer is: How many divine promises were fulfilled in his or her life? Of course, we can ask the question of ourselves at any point.

Use your days

Moses uses an unusual way to describe the length of Abraham's sojourn when he writes about 'the days of the years of Abraham's life' (v. 7). How many days did Abraham live in his 175 years? He lived for about 64,000 days. From another perspective, he had walked with God for a hundred years—for about 36,000 days—which means he had walked in other ways for about 28,000 days. Abraham had lived a great number of days he would have wanted to forget—the days when he worshipped false gods. Yet there were also many days on which he could look back with gladness, days when he had experienced the grace of God. There was the day when the God of glory had appeared to him in Ur of the Chaldees; there was the day when he reached the promised land; there were the days when God protected him, provided for him, pardoned him his faults, promised him great blessings, and spent time with him as his friend.

Yet just as every previous day was born in God's providence, so Abraham's final day dawned. I am sure he anticipated it many times. The account says very little about it other than that he was 'gathered to his people' (v. 8). How many of them there were waiting to greet him cannot be known. Yet down the centuries those who have followed in the footsteps of Abraham the man of faith have found themselves gathered to the same people. Indeed, we are told by Jesus in Matthew 8:11 that 'many will come from east and west and recline at table with Abraham, Isaac, and Jacob in the kingdom of heaven'.

So died the friend of God (Isa. 41:8), who found himself in his Father's house. There he has been for several thousand years enjoying the best of company. The one who looked forward to the day of Christ with gladness (John 8:56) has had a better seat from which to look at the accomplishments of his Saviour. Among them is the fact that the blessing promised to him—the Holy Spirit—has now been given to believers in Jesus (Gal. 3:14). And the father of the faithful is now waiting for the ingathering of God's people so that he, with them, will enter the inheritance promised to him by God (Rom. 4:13).